Knowing the Score

A Guide to Writing College Essays

"Winning through Writing"

Second Edition

Herschel Greenberg

Kendall Hunt
publishing company

Contents

Acknowledgments & Dedication v
Author's Note vii
New for this Edition ix
Introduction xi
    For Students xii
    For Professors xiii

Part 1 Starting the Essay 1
    Chapter 1: Support 3
    Chapter 2: MLA Documentation 15
    Chapter 3: Brainstorming 39
    Chapter 4: Creating a Thesis 49

Part 2 Paragraphs 63
    Chapter 5: Introductions 65
    Chapter 6: Developing Supporting Paragraphs 81
    Chapter 7: Conclusions 97

Part 3 Essay Types 109
    Chapter 8: The Process-Analysis Essay 111
    Chapter 9: The Definition Essay 129
    Chapter 10: Compare and/or Contrast 147
    Chapter 11: The Problem Solution Essay 179
    Chapter 12: The Cause and Effect Essay 211
    Chapter 13: Literary Analysis 237
    Chapter 14: Persuasive Argument 259

Part 4 Further Information 289
    Chapter 15: Formality 291
    Chapter 16: Sentence Meaning 297
    Chapter 17: The In-Class Essay 303

Part 5 Additional Student Essays 315
Activities 367
Appendix 385
Index 401

Acknowledgments & Dedication

I would like to thank my wife, Kathleen, for all of her support and encouragement. I would like to thank my father, Paul, for taking the time to read everything and give me more feedback than I ever thought possible. I also want to thank my mother, Roberta, for taking the time each day to ask me how this book was coming along (the constant reminder kept me focused). Thank you to all my friends and family who took the time to read the different parts of this book (you know who you are). All of your feedback was important and necessary as you helped me shape this book. I would like to thank Jason McFaul for helping me realize a dream of being published and for imparting the wisdom required to see a project from inception to completion. And to everyone at Kendall Hunt—thank you for believing in this project. Finally, I want to thank all of my past students who helped me realize the importance of teaching strong composition skills. Specifically, thank you to all the students who contributed to this book. Your success in my classroom confirmed all of the techniques and strategies used in this book and helped inspire me to put all these ideas on paper.

This book is dedicated to all future students—may you learn the writing skills required to make your college career a success and help you fulfill your goals in life.

Author's Note

I am aware that definitions of key words used in this book differ throughout the academic disciplines. For example, a student in a Philosophy class uses the term *argument* to mean something different than what is used here. Within each chapter, whenever a key word (or an important word) is used, it will also be defined. This way, its context is understood by those who use the book.

In addition, this book refers to all the essay types as argument essays. In doing so, this book states that an argument is formed around a belief—when you write an essay, you are arguing your position. I am aware that it is possible to write an essay based on something you do not believe in. However, in my experience, I find that students who write essays based on something they care about tend to write better essays. That is why most of the essay topics at the end of each chapter are written using general terms. This allows the student to brainstorm and choose his/her own research and essay topic.

Unlike a traditional reader, the student essays used in this book do not come with questions for analysis at the end of the essay. Each essay is designed to be an example of how to apply the techniques learned in the chapter. Any professor can develop questions for class discussion, including ideas about what strengths and weaknesses exist within the sample essay or what techniques were used by the writer.

Finally, the MLA styles used in this book come from the most recent edition of the MLA handbook, *MLA Handbook for Writers of Research Papers, 7th Edition,* released in April 2009. The new edition makes many changes to the format and rules used in the works cited. These rules will be reflected throughout this book. However, some of these rules may contradict previous MLA rules (mostly from the 6th edition), so students and professors need to be aware that MLA does change over time and make adjustments accordingly.

Herschel Greenberg

New for this Edition!

In some ways, writing the second edition was more difficult than writing the first edition. For the second edition, there was so much I wanted to add. However, if I added everything, I risked changing one of the strengths of the book; every chapter is succinct, which makes it easy for students to read and understand. The student feedback for the first edition was amazing. Many students said it was the best English book they have ever read, and many students commented that they saw an improvement in their writing by the end of the semester.

Since the first edition's release, I have had to find new ways to teach composition that complements the book in order to avoid repeating word-for-word what appears on the pages. By doing so, I have realized that there are parts of the book that can be made clearer, and some parts would benefit from an Additional Information section. Therefore, what appears in the second edition is based on those things I have adopted in the classroom. By doing so, this second edition is even stronger while maintaining the same concise and straightforward information and instructions.

Therefore, the second edition now includes the following:

- Many of the early chapters contain an Additional Information section at the end of the chapter. This will help clarify complicated lessons and give extra information that will prove vital in understanding the chapters.
- In particular, the MLA chapter now contains several Additional Information sections in order to help students understand how to use MLA cross-reference correctly.
- In addition, the MLA chapter now contains summarizing instructions.
- Every chapter has more topics and assignments to choose from, including 10 topics for each of the essay chapters. Now, there should be something for everyone.
- There are more student essays—several of the essay chapters now have two student essays. Not only does it help students to see more quality examples, but these essays can lead to students writing their own response.

- A new chapter, called Sentence Meaning, has been added in order to show students how to avoid some of the common errors when writing sentences. This chapter is not about the rules of grammar. It is about how word choice and sentence structure can alter the idea communicated to the reader, which means the writer is not making a clear statement.
- There is an entire section of the book dedicated to activities, including identifying claims, support, and creating an MLA Works Cited.
- Along with the Peer Evaluation, there is a new activity called Self Evaluation. I found this to be a powerful tool in understanding how students write. The information students reveal in the Self Evaluation has greatly affected how I teach composition. And in return, students begin to understand their writing process better, leading to a breakthrough in creating high quality academic papers.
- And finally, new to the second edition is my son, Alexander Muniz Greenberg. He was born shortly before I started work on the second edition, but as a smart and curious baby, he has inspired me to create a book that I hope he will be proud of and someday use himself.

Introduction

Bottom of the 9th...bases are loaded...two outs...full count...the pitch...the swing...

4th quarter, seconds left on the clock...fourth down and inches... The snap...

Recognize these scenarios? They are potential come-from-behind game winners—a thrill of a lifetime.

But these scenarios are only thrilling if we know the score. If neither event is a close game, then the play lacks excitement—the flare that comes with being a sports hero. Knowing the score makes you aware of what is expected of you. Knowing the score makes you prepared to handle any situation and rise to the occasion. Knowing the score will make you a better writer.

In writing, knowing the score means knowing what it takes to write a "winning" essay. This book contains strategies and concepts that will help prepare you to write any of the seven types of essays.

Writing "winning" essays is not difficult; it takes time to master. The purpose of this book is to make that process easier so that you become more comfortable as a writer. This book offers guidelines to help you think through, prepare, and write any kind of essay. There are no formulas here; think of the suggestions in this book as strategies for structuring an essay.

An essay is like a painting—the screen becomes the canvas, the words become the brush. The words on the screen will paint *your* picture. They communicate your thoughts and present your arguments. As each artist has his/her own style, every writer must find his/her own voice. With this in mind, the book is written so as to allow you to choose your own style. Once you learn the fundamentals of how to write "winning" essays, you will be able to create your own masterpiece. Each chapter offers suggestions that fit different styles of writing and different techniques based on the essay assignment. I cannot choose your words. You must think of the words that make the sentences, the sentences that make the paragraphs, and the paragraphs that make up the essay. What I hope to show you is how to put everything together and how to organize your ideas into a "winning" essay.

For Students

Does this sound familiar? You are at your desk, your research is done, and you have your notes. You see the blinking cursor on the white screen that is your word processor. You put your fingers on the keyboard, ready to type, and nothing happens. You watch the cursor in the upper left corner flash. And your fingers do not move. The cursor is mocking you.

I know that feeling, too. It happens to everyone, even the best writers. It is known as "writer's block." The ideas are there, but you do not know what to do with them.

If you have been there and done that, then this book is for you. Even if you find writing essays easy, this book is still for you. It contains tips, hints, techniques, and strategies for writing "winning" essays. For example, **when you are writing an essay, you do not have to start with the first word of the first paragraph of the first page of the essay. Start where you are comfortable.** If you have an argument ready, start there. This is known as *"non-linear writing."* One of the great advantages to word processing is that you are free to move things around and you are free to start anywhere.

There are many kinds of essays, including definition essays, compare and/or contrast essays, and cause and effect essays. This book will cover all of them, and more, with each chapter dedicated to a specific kind of essay. There are ideas and concepts that overlap all the essays types, but the chapters will allow you to study one kind of essay at a time.

Another hint: **you can combine essay types as needed. There is no rule that you must write only one kind of essay—most term papers and research projects employ all the techniques used in this book.** The best essays do this in order to make a more convincing argument (and it makes the essay longer).

I want you to think of this book as a guide, like a handbook or a reference book. I envision you putting this next to your computer so that when you are typing and you have a question on how to do something within the essay, you can use this book to help you. If you are stuck, use the information in this book to help you get "unstuck." If you are given an essay assignment, maybe something from another class completely unrelated to the class you are in now (the one you are using this book for), I want you to be able to use this book to write any kind of essay, for any kind of assignment, for any kind of professor. I want you to know what you need to do to succeed at college writing.

Essentially, I want you to know the score.

For Professors

I am writing this book so that you may use it however you deem best. That is, if you want this to be a supplemental guide that compliments what you already do in the classroom, re-affirming what you teach your students, then this book will do just that. However, if you want to use it as a primary text, then this book is perfect for that, too. Each chapter will have writing prompts, space for brainstorming and thesis writing, and sample student essays. No matter how you use this book, you will find the information to be helpful, informative, and useful.

This book is not a reader. That means you will not find professional essays and articles in this book. I will tell you why: the very first time a student said to me, "Why did I get a low grade? I followed the model in the book," I realized that the problem was not the student's ability to write, but they were imitating the wrong kind of example. Professional writers and journalists do not follow the same formality that I require my students to follow. When I went to look at the essay my student was referring to, I saw that it was full of contractions, first person narratives, and most of the paragraphs had two sentences. I told my class that this essay in the book would probably fail my class! They laughed.

In my opinion, a good essay writing textbook should not contradict what I ask for in my students' essays. If I want them to remove contractions, then they should see examples that do not have contractions. If I ask for a thesis to come at the beginning of their essay (in the introduction), I do not want the professional sample to have their thesis in the conclusion. This contradiction causes confusion amongst students who open the book at home in order to write their essays. The typical essay models used in a reader are flawed because they are written for a different kind of audience using a different set of rules.

This book is about teaching *formal essay writing*. This formality should work across the disciplines. Although this book uses MLA format as its guideline, any of the other documentation styles can be substituted. The important point here is that this book is the foundation for all kinds of college writing, not just English classes.

This is why I have chosen to use student samples in each chapter. I want your students to go home and have something that they can look at in order to see what it takes for them to succeed. If they use this book and see what an "A" paper looks like, then they have a guideline. The student samples in this book meet my criteria of formality and will demonstrate all the techniques learned in that chapter. So when the student is finished reading a chapter on cause and effect, for example, they will find an essay that uses the techniques in the chapter. This will help build the understanding required for writing good essays, and the student samples show how the art of essay writing actually works.

In other words, I want your students to know the score.

PART 1

Starting the Essay

CHAPTER 1

Support

Support is used throughout your essay in order to strengthen your argument. The more accurate and reliable your support, the better your essay will score in class. This chapter will cover the different kinds of support and how to use different research tools. In addition, this chapter will show you how to ask questions about your research in order to determine strong sources from weak sources. Effective essay writers use researched materials to support their position while maintaining their own ideas.

In general, a well-written essay will need at least one piece of support per argument in your essay. We will cover arguments and paragraphs later, but you should think of it like this: I need to learn about my topic before I begin writing about it. Once I know what I am going to write about, I want to find other authors that I can use to prove my points. This means you will want to investigate some kind of support for nearly every paragraph in your essay (introductions and conclusions, which we will cover in other chapters, often do not have support). Examples, definitions, quotes, and statistics are all different kinds of support.

The following deals with the kinds of support acquired through research. We call these kinds of support *outside sources.* An outside source is anything you add to your essay that came from another person. Professors expect you to read different outside sources and use them in your essay (using proper citation).

Factual Evidence

Factual evidence is support based on true, or real, evidence. It is information based on a fact used to support your argument. You will find Factual Evidence in most newspaper articles and magazines that deal with current events. When used as support, Factual Evidence is very powerful and can really boost your argument. There are two categories of factual evidence.

Factual Evidence Based on Statistics

Statistics are those numbers and percentages gathered from raw data, including polls, surveys or some kind of empirical data. Factual evidence usually involves numbers. For example, when a news article talks about X number of people who were affected by a storm, you are seeing Factual Evidence based on Statistics. Or if your teacher asks how many students in the classroom have a job, the ratio created by this answer would be Factual Evidence based on Statistics.

Factual Evidence Based on Example

This is a piece of evidence used as support based on a real example. It is something that really happened, but it not based on stats. This usually involves an example of something real. For example, if a news article talks about the specific damage to a building caused by the storm, that would be Factual Evidence based on Example. Or, if a specific student discussed his/her job, that would be Factual Evidence based on Example.

Opinions: Interpretations of the Facts

If we took a poll in your class based on the number of students that work while going to school, we would get a specific number of people. That is a fact and would not be disputed. However, the *interpretation* of that fact can be argued. What does it mean that X number of you work and go to school? How do we analyze that information? This is where opinions come into play, and it is your job to decipher good information from bad information when doing research. You need to look at several important factors in order to determine whether or not a source is reliable enough to use in your essay. The following are different types of opinions.

Interpretation Based on Expert Opinion

This is the most common kind of opinion most of you will encounter. It is when an expert makes some kind of argument based on facts. Your job is to determine what makes someone an expert. If you are looking into genetic alterations, then look at who is making the argument. Is it a grad student from Berkeley? Or is it a doctor with a PhD in genetics who has been practicing for twenty years? One is more of an authority than the other, and you need to take this into consideration when looking at interpretations and arguments. Remember, the fact that someone is an expert in a particular area does not automatically make his/her opinion correct. The opinion still needs to be supported by evidence. When you do research, you want to evaluate why that person is an expert and if they are qualified to give an opinion.

Interpretation Based on Causal Connection

When we talk about cause and effect, we are making a claim that there is a direct causal relation between two events. For example, if science has proven that a cold is caused by a virus, we would need evidence of this. However, when an author offers an opinion on what a cold can do to you mentally and physically (or how it can affect your job, your relationship, etc.), you are witnessing the argument based on causal connection. You are to examine the author's argument that there is a correlation between two events. Once you have established the correlation, your job is to determine whether or not the author makes a valid connection. It is often the case that faulty assumptions are made about the causal connection between two events.

Interpretation Based on Solutions to Problems

Solutions to problems are also arguments and usually occur after statistics or examples reveal that there is a problem. A proposed solution constitutes an argument because it is someone's position—they are claiming that his/her solution will work. When you encounter this kind of argument, your job is to look at the truth of the evidence and the validity of the argument being made. Is the problem real? Is the solution reasonable? These are the kinds of things you should be thinking about when you find opinions based on this kind of argument.

Interpretation Based on Predictions of the Future

Sometimes experts make predictions (and offer opinions) about the future based on factual evidence. They are predicting what might happen. Your job is to determine the degree of probability of that prediction being true. Remember, you can get true predictions from false information. You want to examine both the evidence used to make the prediction and whether or not the prediction is reasonable.

Once you have found the information you want to use in your essay, you need to ask yourself some questions. By doing this, you are trying to find the best support possible. The better the support from our outside sources, the more it will help your argument in your essay.

Evaluating Factual Evidence

1. Is the evidence up-to-date?
2. Is the evidence sufficient?
3. Is the evidence relevant?
4. Do the statistics come from trustworthy sources?
5. Are the terms of the statistics clearly defined?
6. Has any significant information been omitted?

Evaluating factual evidence is important. For example, pretend that you are doing research for an essay, and an article claims that teenage pregnancy (teenagers in high school) has dropped over the past five years. Now, 12% of high school teenagers get pregnant, but five years ago, that number was 15% (I am making this up in order to illustrate a point.) Here are a series of questions you should immediately begin asking yourself. Who took this poll? What was their objective? Why has the percentage dropped over the years? How many students were polled? Certain parts of the country have higher or lower rates based on many different factors, so it is very important to understand the location of the poll.

Evaluating Opinions

1. Is the source qualified to give an opinion?
2. Does the source have a bias?
3. Has the source used sufficient evidence to support his/her claim?
4. Is the source's argument logical?
5. How recent is the opinion? Recent facts can change people's opinions.

Using the same example from your research on teenage pregnancy, suppose the article you are reading offers an opinion based on that data. What is the basis for that author's opinion? What questions do you have about how the author made that argument? For example, what about the other 88% of the students? Does that mean 88% are not having sex? Or are they having protected sex, and therefore, not getting pregnant? Has sex education in freshman studies contributed to a larger number of students not having sex at such a young age? Teenage pregnancy statistics can have many uses, and you must look at the context and purpose in order to understand their meaning. For example, politicians can use surveys and polls for many different reasons, and nearly any result can be interpreted however it is needed.

What happens if you do not verify your source and use it as support anyway? Imagine a professor reads your essay and you use a statistic from twenty years ago.

The professor will know this information is outdated not only because common sense tells the professor that things have changed, but because that professor just read an article in a magazine that reveals a new argument based on the new statistical information. The argument you are trying to make in your essay is now weaker. Your support did not help your essay—it actually hurt your argument. New statistical information can lead to a conclusion different from the one you argued. That is why verifying your source is so important. You need to make sure the person, example, or factual evidence you find is the absolute best and most accurate information available. Good support and good arguments means you will have a good essay.

Where do you find this support, you ask? You find sources for support in books, journals, newspapers, and even the Internet.

Books

Books are your most valuable asset. Your campus library is full of books waiting for you to explore. If you are unfamiliar with your campus library, I would suggest you walk in and take a tour. Most libraries offer short sessions, tours, or classes that teach you how to use all of the library's tools. That can be very useful information to have throughout your college career.

There are so many books, how does one start looking for sources? You use the library's database (card catalogs are now online), so you should begin by searching for your topic. Type in what you want to learn about for your essay. Once you have a list, you need to physically go to the stacks and find your books. Yes, most students fear this, but you do need to get the books off the shelves and look at them.

What are you looking for exactly? This is a very important question you should be asking yourself. The best way to explain this is to use an example.

Suppose your assignment is to write about some of the issues involving immigration in America today. Your topic is wide open because your professor did not ask you for something specific. You are free to develop your own specific topic inside the given parameters.

Drive (or walk) to the library. On the way there, you have a good feeling about this topic, and you have decided that you are really interested in researching about immigration and Southern California. By making this decision, you have already helped yourself narrow the number of books you need to look at.

Once at the library, begin your search. Type in something like this: "immigration California." This will generate a long list of books.

Now, this is an important hint: when you see all of those books, do not be alarmed. Instead, I want you to judge a book by its title (this is contrary to the saying that you should not judge a book by its cover). You have to do this; otherwise, you will be going home with hundreds of books. Look at the titles of the books in the list. Which ones focus on Southern California? Do you see any titles that interest you? If you do, these are the titles you should focus on. In addition, inside the list of books, you should see copyright dates and authors. Remember what to do when evaluating a source—if a book you are looking at has the title, *Immigration Statistics,* but was published in 1973, the book might not work for you.

Once you have judged the books by their titles, you need to go get those books. The next step you need to do is open the books to their table of contents. Look at the chapter names and examine how each book is constructed. Flip to a chapter that you think might help you and do a quick read of that chapter. Does it look like it has good information? If the answer is yes, then you are going to take that book home.

The important thing to remember here is that you do not want to go home with fifty books. Not only is that heavy and a lot to carry, but you cannot possibly read fifty books! The more you can narrow-down your topic and look at the book in the library, the less you will carry home. And this way, you can focus on reading the books that will help your essay. You want to focus on the books that give you the most support!

Journals and Articles

When you did that search for immigration in California, you may have noticed other things were listed besides books. Library databases also contain scholarly journals. These journals are usually published by universities and contain academic essays. Each journal focuses on a theme. You may have found a journal about immigration through a literature perspective. These journals make great sources as well. They are current, and the people published inside of them are often other professors who are passionate about the topic of the journal.

The essays in these journals are similar to the essays you write. They will have a clear thesis and good arguments, and the writer has oftentimes already done the very research you are just starting. So here is a secret: if you find an essay in a journal, you should read it and look at the author's notes at the end (it will be called a Works Cited or Bibliography). Look at those sources! Did you notice how they were used in the essay? The reason this is important is because you just discovered many new sources for your topic. It is a great way to continue to develop your research skills.

Because journals are often published several times a year, a library cannot keep the entire collection on the shelf. When this happens, the journals are usually put on microfilm—an easier way to store what would be hundreds of journals. However, many journals now appear on the Internet. Most campus libraries will have access to databases containing journals. If you have never used microfilm or the databases at your library, be sure to ask a librarian for help.

Besides journals, you may want to use current events as a source in your essay. For this, it is best to look in newspapers and magazines for articles pertaining to your topic. For example, *Time Magazine* is a great source for news and current events. If you are looking at immigration in Southern California, you may find an article about a new law that just passed. This kind of information is so recent you will not find it in books or journals. You will need to rely on newspapers. Most libraries have the larger newspapers that are in circulation, and many libraries have back issues as well. This is a valuable source to be aware of because oftentimes current events can really help support an argument in your essay.

Internet

Most students know how to use the Internet. An entire generation of students have relied on the Internet for research. Although it has not replaced a trip to the library, it is an excellent tool for doing research. Nothing can replace books and journals, but if you are willing to verify your sources and double-check everything, the Internet can be very useful.

The biggest problem with the Internet is its size—there is actually too much information! Type "immigration California" into your favorite search engine, and you might get over 500,000 different websites!

The other problem with doing Internet research is that nearly anyone has the power to write something online. It can be an opinion, a blog (a web log), or a message on the bulletin board. This is where those questions about your sources come in handy. You really need to check who is saying what and where they are saying it when it comes to using the Internet.

The good news is that, like a book, you can sometimes gain information by looking at the website's URL address. For example, a .gov, .edu, or .org tend to be better and more reliable websites than a .com. If you are looking for government statistics on the number of reported immigrants that came to California, using a .gov website should prove reliable.

Another asset to doing research online is a website like Amazon.com. You can use Amazon.com to look up a book without leaving your house. There may be books you see online that are not in your campus library. Sometimes, using a website like Amazon.com will help you determine what books to look for in your campus library because you can read the title and sometimes read the first few pages online.

All of the tips in this chapter are designed to help you find support. You need to tell the difference between good support and bad support. You also need to be able to determine what kind of support helps your essay and what kind of support does not. You need to learn to find a balance in relation to the amount of time you research compared to the amount of time you spend writing. All of this takes practice, and you will get better at it with time. But now you know the score because you have learned what kind of support exists and where to find it.

Additional Information

1. Books contain some of the most reliable information. However, books can also contain outdated information. Be careful of books with old copyright information.

2. Journals and articles contain reliable information that is also current. However, they are often harder to find and may appear as "news" rather than arguments for support.

3. The Internet has the most recent information because it is updated regularly. However, it is the least reliable because anyone can post anything on a web page. In addition, it is possible to be overwhelmed by the amount of material available for review. When using the web, you have to be diligent and check your information for accuracy.

CHAPTER 1 ACTIVITIES

Try finding sources on the following topics. You should find two books, two journals or articles and two Internet sources for each topic. You can make the topic as general or specific as you want.

1. Immigration

2. Homelessness

3. Racism

4. Sports

5. Politics

6. Economics

Name: _____   Date: _____

Sources

_____

_____

_____

_____

_____

_____

_____

_____

_____

_____

_____

_____

_____

_____

_____

_____

_____

CHAPTER 2

MLA Documentation

In the previous chapter, we discussed how to find and analyze support. Once you have found the support you are looking for, there are rules to follow when you use that support in your essay. In the English discipline, we use something called MLA documentation. MLA stands for Modern Language Association, and this chapter will focus on how to do MLA correctly. There are other formats, like APA and Chicago, that other disciplines use, but for your English classes, you will need to know the correct MLA style. The current format can be found in the new 7th edition released in April 2009 and will be used throughout this book.

There are many rules in MLA—so many, in fact, that it is not possible to discuss all of them here. This chapter only contains a few types of sources you might use. That is why the people that make MLA wrote a reference book (*MLA Handbook for Writers of Research Papers, 7th Edition*). This is something that all professors would recommend you own. This chapter will give you many of the rules that make up the foundation of MLA, but there are things that will be left out and you might need that information for your essay. That is why the MLA reference book is very important. If you cannot memorize a rule, you will at least know where to find the answer.

MLA is designed to make your essay clean and readable. You use documentation in order to give credit to the source you use. Any information or quote you gather from an outside source needs to be documented because if you do not, you may be plagiarizing. Plagiarizing occurs when you fail to give credit to a source of information or idea on any written work submitted for academic purposes. When you use a direct statement, the words taken directly from the written (or oral) work must be placed in quotation marks with the appropriate reference cited. When you paraphrase and summarize someone else's ideas, you must also use appropriate citation. By using MLA correctly, you are giving credit to your source. Documenting your source correctly will let your reader know exactly where you found the information in your essay and who wrote it (or said it, or researched it, or thought it). The goal of MLA is to clearly label and identify where you found your sources so your reader can find them, too.

MLA also wants your paper to look a certain way. Therefore, you should set your word processing program to be Times New Roman font, 12 point font size, double-spaced, and your text should be printed on white paper with black ink. Your margins should be one inch on all sides. You want every page to be numbered (including the Works Cited page) with your last name next to the page number.

MLA breaks down into two parts. First, there is the documentation in your essay. There are rules to follow about how to document a source as you type. Second, there is something called a "works cited." This is where you list all the sources you used in your essay. This is different than a Bibliography, which gives you a list of all the books read by an author of an essay or recommended by the author of the essay. It does not mean that those sources were actually used in the essay. In MLA, we create a works cited because it shows the reader only those sources used in your essay. This allows someone reading your essay to trace exactly what you used as support. This way, someone can read the source material for him/herself.

Again, MLA is all about making your documentation clear within the essay. So we are going to start there.

Part 1: Documentation Inside the Essay

MLA requires two very important pieces of information inside your essay. **You will need the author of your source and the page number where the quote came from (in order to begin demonstrating how this works, we will assume that you are using a book as a source and that you have something you want to quote).** Once you have this information, MLA has many options to choose from when you type your essay. For example, you can use something called "parenthetical notation," which is a specific location to put information at the end of the sentence.

In the following examples, we will look at a book by Ayn Rand called *Anthem*.

Example #1

Rand writes, "Then we slept. The sleeping halls were white and clean and bare of all things save one hundred beds" (21).

Did you notice the information MLA requires? The author's name appears at the beginning of the sentence. The page number appears in the *parenthetical notation* (the parenthesis at the end of the sentences contains MLA). Using this method makes your documentation clear and easy to read.

Here are a few important things to note. First, when you refer to an author for the very first time in your essay, you write his/her entire name. So the first time you mention the author of the book in the example, you would write "Ayn Rand." Then, every time after that, you would just write "Rand." This shows the proper respect to the author you are quoting.

Second, notice the word *writes*. You use this word in the present tense because of how MLA views a book—it is something that continues to exist in time, in the present, even though it was written in the past. The words are there on the page today. The author did not speak these words, so you would use the word "writes."

Third, notice the page number that appears in the parenthesis. It does not say (page 21) or (p21) or (#21). It simply says (21). MLA does not want anything other than the page number. If this quote started on the bottom of page 21 and continued onto page 22, you would still write (21). Students love to get creative with their page numbers. Remember, MLA just wants the number and nothing else.

Fourth, notice where the period ends the sentence. Yes, that is correct; the parenthetical notation is part of your sentence. The period comes at the end of the parenthesis, even if the sentence you are quoting ends in a period. This is important to remember.

Finally, **quotes cannot stand alone.** This means that you must introduce the quote. What is inside the quote does not constitute your words or ideas. They are someone else's words and ideas. In order to make it your sentence, you must write something before it, to introduce it somehow. In the example given, stating "Rand writes" does exactly that.

So what happens if you get tired of writing "Rand writes" throughout your essay? Remember, as long as you have the necessary information, MLA is flexible.

Example #2

She writes, "Then we slept. The sleeping halls were white and clean and bare of all things save one hundred beds" (Rand 21).

Notice the difference? Instead of beginning the sentence with the author's last name, it is now in the parenthetical notation. Look closely at how it is formatted. It goes author's last name, space, then the page number. The period still ends the parenthesis, thus ending your sentence. This makes it clean and easy to read.

What happens if you have more than one book by the same author? MLA allows for a third piece of information in the sentence—the title of the book.

Example #3

According to the book *Anthem*, "And we sighed, as if a burden had been taken from us" (Rand 44).

Or

Rand writes, "And we sighed, as if a burden had been taken from us" (*Anthem* 44).

Now notice how the title of the book is used in the sentence. It is in two different places in the examples above. Either way, it is clear who the author is, which book you are referring to and what page number the quote can be found on.

What happens if the quote you are using is spoken dialogue between characters in a story?

Example #4

Equality said, "'The Council does not know of this hole, so it cannot be forbidden'" (Rand 31).

In this case, you can reference the name of the character instead of the author at the beginning of your sentence. However, the parenthetical notation still contains the information you need—the author and the page number.

However, you will notice something different within the quotes. These are called *single quotes.* You use single quotes whenever the sentence(s) you are quoting has quotes around them, including dialogue or something the author added on their own. The double quote is yours—it tells the reader exactly where your quote begins and ends. The single quote tells the reader that the thing you are quoting was also in quotes. Again, be sure to notice how everything is formatted.

If you do not want to use parenthetical notation, or you simply want to use various formatting techniques, MLA allows you to choose how to format your quote.

Example #5

On page 45, Rand writes, "...sitting here in our tunnel, we wonder about these words.

It is forbidden, not to be happy...all men must be happy."

Here, everything MLA requires is in the sentence itself instead of at the end in the parenthetical notation. MLA is flexible in this way—you can choose how to format a sentence.

You should have also noticed something else in Example #5. See those three dots? We call those *ellipses.* They have a very specific purpose in MLA writing. When you quote something that is very long, you often do not want to quote every sentence. For example, if you are looking at quoting a paragraph, you may only want the first few sentences and the last sentence, removing the sentences in between. The job of the ellipses is to tell the reader that you are omitting material from the quote. This is very useful because you can remove sentences and words to make your point. Again, this is often necessary for long quotes.

Ellipses can be used to remove words or sentences by telling the reader that there is something more that exists in the original source, but you are choosing to remove it. Because of this, ellipses can come at the beginning, middle, or end of a quote. Again, look at Example #5, and you can see how it was used. If you go to page 45 in Rand's book, you will find more to the sentences than appears here.

MLA also has a strategy for when you do quote something very long. If your quote is four or more lines (this means four or more of your typed lines, not the lines from your source), you indent (double Tab) the block of text to distinguish it from everything else. You use a colon after you introduce the quote instead of quotation marks, and the parenthetical notation goes outside of the period. The quote needs to be double-spaced like everything else. The following is a good example of how to format a paragraph with a long quote.

Example #6

In 1978, Cultural Theorist Edward Said wrote a book called *Orientalism,* which started to examine how Western Culture defined different cultures in relation to itself. He looked at the region we call the "Orient" (which is actually the Middle East region). In his book, Said makes the claim that the concept of the Orient is entirely defined by Western Culture. This concept includes how we view and understand their social norms, political behavior, and world views, which then permeates our society through the various forms of media and education. It is an exercise in the "Will to Power" of Western Culture over the Orient which defines and affects how we perceive these people; in affect, making our culture acceptable and desirable and the "other" culture unacceptable and undesirable. Said writes:

> It is rather a *distribution* of geopolitical awareness into aesthetic scholarly, economic, sociological, historical, and philological texts, it is an *elaboration* not only of a basic geographical distinction but also of a whole series of "interests" which, by such means as scholarly discovery, philological reconstruction, psychological analysis, landscape and sociological description, it not only creates but also maintains; it is, rather than expresses, a certain will or *intention* to understand, in some cases control, manipulate, even to incorporate, what is a manifestly different world; it is, above all, a discourse that is by no means in direct, corresponding relationship with political power in the raw but rather is produced and exists in an uneven

> exchange with various kinds of power, shaped to a degree by the
>
> exchange with power political..., power intellectual..., power
>
> cultural..., and power moral. (12)

In essence, the suppressed culture is unaware of the mandates by the dominate

culture because the suppressed culture does not view themselves the same way.

Hence, the suppressed culture does not attempt to affect change through

communication, text, and media with the dominant culture and therefore, the

concept of the "other" culture is never rectified.

Works Cited

Said, Edward W. *Orientalism.* New York: Vintage Books, 1979. Print.

I know that is one long quote, but you need to notice all the things that make it different than a normal quote. Notice the colon after "Said writes" and notice that in this situation, the period that ends your sentence comes before the parenthetical notation. You should notice that the quotation marks disappear when you use this format. You should also notice how much distance two tabs create. This really off-sets your quote so that the reader knows that the block of text that appears is a source you are quoting.

Another way to add a source to your essay is by using *summarizing*. Summarizing is defined as something you write when you put a source's argument in your own words. It is the core idea from an author's argument rewritten in your essay. When summarizing, you must cite the source using the MLA documentations methods used in this chapter. However, a summary does not need a page number, since you are not referencing a specific page.

You need to reference the source because the original idea does not belong to you, even though what you wrote appears using your own words. Sometimes, an author's argument is too long or too complex, so summarizing helps you insert an outside source without a direct quote.

A summary can be one sentence or many sentences. In addition, you have the choice where to put the reference, just like a direct quote. When you use a summary, you want to distinguish the summary of someone else's argument from the rest of your paper. In the examples below, the MLA reference makes it clear what exactly is being summarized.

Example #7

In her book, she argues that individualism will always be a better choice than living in utopian societies (Rand).

Or

Rand also argues that what we give up in civil liberties, we gain back in equality and safety. However, Rand warns that if we give up critical thinking, we jeopardize the very core of what makes us human.

Additional Information: Documentation Inside the Essay

1. MLA requires the following cross-reference used inside the essay:
   A. Author's last name (either in the sentence or in the parenthesis)
   B. A page number (if applicable—websites often lack page numbers)
   C. Title of work if necessary (this is required if the source lacks an author)

Use this as a checklist to make sure you are using MLA correctly.

2. You must introduce quotes with words that belong to you in order to make a complete sentence. In addition to the examples given in #1–#5, here are a few additional templates for starting a sentence, where X is an author or a title used in the sentence:
   A. According to X
   B. X argues
   C. As supported by X
   D. X himself/herself writes
   E. In X's opinion

Keep in mind that the author or title can go either in the sentence or in the parenthesis at the end of the sentence.

3. When you introduce an author for the first time, try to establish who that person is and why they are qualified to give a quote in your essay.
4. *Books, Movies, Newspapers, Magazines, Journals, and Website Names go in italics.*
5. "Essays, print articles, web articles, poems, and short stories go in quotes."
6. If you use a direct quote, you need to have quotation marks at the beginning and the end of the direct quote.
7. Often, you will encounter an essay written by an author that uses another person as support. In this case, MLA does not need you to track down the original source of the quote. Instead, give credit to the person who made the argument, but reference the author where you found the quote. For example, Smith argues, "The sky is blue" (Graff 77). This implies that a person named Smith made an argument used in Graff's essay on page 77. The cross-reference here is Graff, which means the Works Cited gives credit to the essay Graff wrote.
8. Summaries need an author for reference. Even if you describe something, like a scene in a movie or the plot in a book, it needs the correct MLA reference. If you do not have an author, your summary needs to reference the Works Cited using the title.

Part 2: Creating a Works Cited

Once you have used a quote from a source in your essay, you need to create something called a works cited. This is a list of all the sources you used in your essay. This list goes at the end of your essay.

There are many, many types of sources you can use in research. What we will discuss here is only a small portion of the things you might encounter. It is important to know the basic ideas and principals used by MLA. So we will start with a simple entry.

The **basic entry (single author of a book)** follows this format.

Last Name, First Name. *Title*. Publication Information. Format.

Notice the periods. There must be a period after each part of the source. You should not think of them as periods—they are dividing marks between the four key elements required for documentation. The title must be italicized (books, movies, newspapers, magazines, and journals are italicized. Poems, essays, and article titles go in quotes). If we expand the publication information, it would look like this:

Last Name, First Name. *Title*. Publication location: Publication Company,

      copyright. Print.

Notice the colon and the comma. These belong in the publication information. Here are some tips: if your source has more than one publication location, you choose the location closest to where you live. Also, if there is more than one copyright date (which is often) you choose the most recent. You want to identify the exact book you got your information from. Finally, current MLA rules state that you need to use words such as "Print," "Web," "Film," and "DVD" based on the medium of the source. This information will always go at the end.

Below is an example of the book by Ayn Rand. It is formatted correctly and is necessary if you use a quote from the book.

Rand, Ayn. *Anthem*. New York: Signet, 1995. Print.

Also, when you create a works cited, it starts on its own page. It should have the number in the upper-right corner like all your other pages and should also have your last name. A works cited is arranged in **alphabetical order,** usually by author's last name. If you have a title or something else, then it still follows in alphabetical order. In addition, when a source in the works cited goes to a second line, you need to tab it in to make it appear as one unit. When you are all done with your sources, you need to double space the entire thing.

Here are some other sample entries you might need. Remember, they all follow the basic entry stated above.

If you have an essay or article written by someone inside a source written by someone else, you use an **anthology** entry. In this case, you are giving credit to the author of the essay first. Then, give credit to the author or editor of the book. You will notice that the title of the book is italicized, but the title of the essay is in quotes. In addition, unlike a book entry (see previous), an essay in an anthology needs the starting page and ending page of the entire essay. This is the correct format:

Johnston, Ray. "An Essay About Ayn Rand." *The World Literature Anthology*. Ed.

    Jane Smith. New York: Penguin Press, 2007. 201–223. Print.

When using a **scholarly journal with an essay** inside it, it is similar to a book and an anthology. The difference comes when the journal has a volume and issue number. You write the volume and issue number as two numbers separated by a period, with the first number being the volume and the second number being the issue. You then put the year the journal was published in parenthesis, and you must include the page numbers of the entire essay. You include this here so the reader knows how long the essay was, but you include the actual page number used inside your essay. Here is an example:

Feldman, Mark. "Remember Whitman's War." *Walt Whitman Quarterly Review*

      23.1 (2005): 1–25. Print.

Students often use **dictionaries** when doing research. Since dictionaries are compiled by many different people and the dictionary's title usually dictates publication information, MLA has simplified the citing of a dictionary.

"Leader." *Webster's New World Dictionary.* 3rd ed. 1991. Print.

When using a **newspaper article,** most of the same rules apply. The date is written in a different order, and if there is a section number, you need to include that as well. If the article continues on another page, then you write the start page and include a "+". In the example that follows, "A1" implies the article is only on page 1. "A1+" means the article starts on page 1 and continues on another page.

Smith, Joseph. "Gas Prices are on the Rise." *L.A. Times* 22 Oct. 2007: A1. Print.

If you watch a **movie,** this is how you would write it in the works cited. Write "Dir." for the word *director,* and state the major actors by starting with "Perf.", which means "performance." If you are citing a DVD, then continue the entry with the publication information for the DVD, including the year it was released (DVDs can be different from the movies shown in the theater). Finally, end with the word "Film" for movies seen in the theater or "DVD" for movies watched on DVD.

Star Wars: A New Hope. Dir. George Lucas. Perf. Harrison Ford, Carrie Fisher, and

      Mark Hamill. 20th Century Fox, 1977. Film.

Or

Star Wars: A New Hope. Dir. George Lucas. Perf. Harrison Ford, Carrie Fisher, and

Mark Hamill. 1977. 20th Century Fox, 2008. DVD.

The 7th edition of the MLA Handbook made several changes to the rules for citing **websites.** The problem with citing an Internet source is the diversity in which websites exist—they can have authors, compilers, webmasters, article titles, web page titles, website titles, and can change from one day to the next. There are so many kinds of websites that it would be impossible to talk about all of them here.

For the most part, you will need to gather as much information as possible. This means you will need to investigate the website to find the information required in a citation. In general, a website with no author, date, or publication information should be treated with some skepticism (see Chapter 1). Doing research requires finding good, reliable sources, and many websites without this information can be proven unreliable.

In addition, the MLA rules have asked that you remove the URL web link from the entry in the works cited (URLs often change or are too long to type into a browser). The web link is only used when the reader of your essay will have trouble finding your source. For example, if your source lacks an author, then the URL would be included. If the source lacks a title, then the URL will be included. But if you have all the information needed, do not include the URL.

The basic method used for a website will follow this order:

1. Name of author, compiler (often a group that manages the website), or editor
2. "Title of the work or article in quotes"
3. *Name of the overall web site in italics* (this is usually found on the top of the page, or upper left corner. It is the name of the site, not the URL)
4. Publisher or sponsor of the website (this is who owns the site and can usually be found on the bottom of the web page next to the publication date. This is similar to the information of a publisher for a book. It will sometimes be different than the site name)
5. Date of publication (put a comma between the publisher and the date like a book)
6. Medium of publication (in this case, write the word "Web")
7. Date you viewed the website
8. Include the entire URL only if necessary. A web link goes inside < >. Only include this if you lack the information in numbers 1–4 above. Otherwise, leave it out.

In the following example, the article can be found on the *Los Angeles Times* website. Notice how it is formatted and meets all of the requirements. You do not need to include the URL for the website because this article is easy to find with the information given.

Lopez, Robert. "Protestors Rally in Hermosa Beach Against Tax Hikes."

> *Los Angeles Times.* Los Angeles Times, 12 Apr. 2009. Web. 20 Apr. 2009.

In the previous example, I had all the information I needed to create the entry in the works cited. If the article did not have an author, I would start with the title. If the particular website did not state the name of the company or sponsor of the website (#4 in the list) I would have to leave it out. MLA is flexible in this way—the more information you can give, the easier it will be for someone to find your source. For example, many colleges have databases that contain scholarly journals. Writing *Project Muse* or *JSTOR* after the publication information (and before "Web") will tell the reader where you got the information.

A website is not that different from the other types of entries. It contains an author, a title, a specific location, and all the copyright information. If you can remember the general order MLA requires, you will have no problem generating entries in your works cited for other kinds of sources.

Additional Information: Creating a Works Cited

Use the following information as a checklist to verify your Works Cited.

1. A Works Cited needs a title in the center of the page called Works Cited.
2. A Works Cited goes in alphabetical order no matter what. This includes author's last name and titles of sources. MLA follows normal alphabetizing rules.
3. A Works Cited must be double-spaced. In fact, everything in MLA is double-spaced.
4. A Works Cited follows MLA formatting rules, including Times New Roman and 12-point font.
5. A Works Cited must go on its own page. It is also sequentially numbered in terms of the rest of the essay.
6. MLA now requires a code word to end the entry. This code word tells the reader how you viewed the source. Use words like Print, Web, Film, DVD, CD, Radio, and Television to clarify the source.

7. MLA requires the date to be written as Day (two digits), Month (standard abbreviation) and Year (written out fully). For example, it should be written as 29 Aug. 2009. Here is how the months should appear in the Works Cited: Jan. Feb. Mar. Apr. May June July Aug. Sept. Oct. Nov. Dec.

8. Websites create problems because of inconsistencies between different sites. In general, use a web source that has all of the information needed to make a web entry. If that source lacks the information needed, you should be skeptical and consider using a different website. Once you make your Works Cited entry using the techniques for websites, verify that it works by tracking down the article yourself. If it takes you longer than 30 seconds to find the source, there is probably something wrong with the information given in the Works Cited.

Part 3: Checking the Cross Reference

Do you remember why MLA exists? You need to make sure that your *cross reference* between your documented essay and your works cited is correct. Cross reference means that if you give a quote and refer to an author by his/her last name, then your works cited entry begins with that author's last name. Look at my first five examples and how I referenced Rand. Then, in my first full MLA entry, I give you the information about Rand's book. This is correct cross reference.

Cross referencing for books is easy. It gets trickier for more complex journals and Internet articles. For example, if your website does not have an author, but does have a title, this becomes your cross reference. For example, this could be a sentence in your essay:

According to an Internet article, ". . . gas prices will greatly affect the economy in many ways" ("Gas Prices are on the Rise").

If so, this would be your works cited entry:

"Gas Prices are on the Rise." *CNN*. Cable News Network, 23 Oct. 2007. Web. 27 Nov. 2008.

Do you see the cross reference? The title referenced in your sentence is the beginning point for your entry. This is very important in MLA.

There is a lot to learn in this chapter, and MLA takes practice. It is not something you learn to do overnight. But now you have seen it in action, and by the time you are done doing assignments with this book, you will have had plenty of practice. But when it comes to MLA, at least now you know the score.

Additional Information: Checking the Cross-Reference

1. Cross-reference is very important because it is how your reader finds the information in your Works Cited based on your source that you used in your essay.
2. If you have an author, you **must** use the author's last name as the cross-reference.
3. If you do not have an author, you **must** use the title as the cross-reference. This is very common for web sources.
4. The complete title must be used both in the essay and in the Works Cited. Remember, article titles go in quotes, even those found on the Internet. This means you need to put quotes around the title in the essay **and** in the Works Cited.
5. Always check the spelling of the author's name you use. This is important in order to avoid confusion on the correct spelling of an author.
6. You can always verify your MLA cross-reference by matching what you wrote in your essay compared to what starts the entry in the Works Cited.

CHAPTER 2 ACTIVITIES

Now it is time to put all of this into practice. Using the same topics from Chapter 1, you should have gathered some sources. Now use those sources to create a works cited and write sentences containing quotes. You do not need to write a paragraph—just write a quote and the corresponding works cited. Here is the list of topics again:

1. Immigration

2. Homelessness

3. Racism

4. Sports

5. Politics

6. Economics

Name: _____   Date: _____

Brainstorm

_____

_____

_____

_____

_____

_____

_____

_____

_____

_____

_____

_____

_____

_____

_____

_____

_____

_____

_____

Name: _____   Date: _____

Quotes

_____

_____

_____

_____

_____

_____

_____

_____

_____

_____

_____

_____

_____

_____

_____

_____

_____

_____

Name: _____   Date: _____

Works Cited

_____

_____

_____

_____

_____

_____

_____

_____

_____

_____

_____

_____

_____

_____

_____

_____

_____

_____

_____

CHAPTER 3

Brainstorming

Students often say that they will stare at the computer screen for hours before typing the first word. "It is like that flashing cursor is mocking me," they say. Part of the writing process requires that you gather your thoughts, ideas, and examples before you even put a word on the screen. That is why brainstorming helps organize your essay, including your main arguments and paragraphs within the essay. Brainstorming helps get ideas that are in your head onto paper. So before you even begin typing, consider putting ideas about your topic on paper.

There are many forms of brainstorming that we will discuss in this chapter. There is no correct brainstorming method, so choose the one you are most comfortable with. Ultimately, as long as you do something that helps you get started, you are taking the right step.

Many professors will want to see your brainstorm. This will help a professor analyze the early phases of your writing. Even if a professor does not require that you show your brainstorm, it is a good idea to do one anyway. Even the best writers need to start somewhere, and the brainstorm is the best place to start.

1) Listing

The first method is called the **listing.** Simply take all the ideas you have about one topic and put them on a piece of paper. This is a good way to see exactly what information you have to work with. Once you have created the list, go back through the list and find topics that you want to write about. For example, pretend an assignment asks you to write about "cars." You could create a list like this:

CARS
_____

Brand names

Names of specific models

Color

Speed

Safety

MPG

Price of car

Insurance

Type (SUV, Truck, Sedan)

After-market parts

Cost to maintain

Environmental impact

By no means is this list complete. It would simply get your ideas onto paper. Once you have started your list, go back and look at the list again. What interests you in terms of writing a paper? Perhaps you want to explore the environmental impact of cars, relating the MPG with the cost of gas today. Or maybe you want to argue that cars are very expensive to own and require responsibilities many people do not consider. Either way, once you have the list, you can draw out ideas that are connected in order to help organize your thoughts.

2) Cluster/Spider-web/Popcorn

This method has many names, often referred to as a **cluster or spider-web.** I often call it a "popcorn brainstorm," because once you start connecting ideas, things begin to pop (and the end result looks like a piece of popcorn). Many of you have used this method before in other writing classes. You put the topic you are required to write about in the middle of the page and put a circle around it. Then put several other circles and link them to your main topic. Inside each of those circles write down what comes to your mind that relates to the topic. Like the list method, the goal is to get all of your ideas organized on paper before you begin writing. Continue to branch off ideas as your cluster grows. For example, let us say an assignment asks you to write about "pets." That is a very large topic that can be made simpler by using this kind of brainstorm.

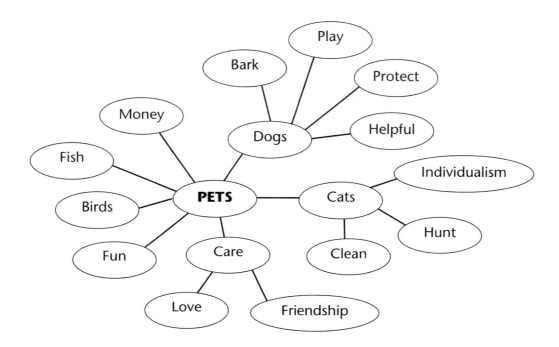

When a brainstorm is this big, it is a good idea to choose the topics you are most interested in and re-brainstorm the new topic. You will often find yourself having new ideas pop into your head about specific topics once you are done with the initial brainstorm. For example, once I see my "pets" brainstorm, I might choose to focus on dogs, requiring a new brainstorm. This will help you get ready for writing an essay.

3) Free Write

Another method is called **free writing.** Many students have ideas on what they want to write about, but they do not know where to begin. A free write is simply a string of ideas explaining to yourself what you are going to write about. In a free write, you do not need to worry about punctuation and spelling. Just write, and keep writing until you have nothing left to say. Many of you know this technique as "stream of consciousness." However, since the free write requires you to have some ideas before you begin writing, many of you may find this technique more useful after you have brainstormed using another method. For example, look at the topic of "pets" in order to see how a brainstorm like this might differ from the cluster method.

I like pets they make me happy I own a cat and a dog they get along together I can walk my dog but I cannot walk my cat She is independent and only lets me pet her when she wants my dog is so much fun we take him to the park to play every weekend and he is even trained to listen to commands I like both of my pets but my dog is more fun to play with Im responsibly for cleaning up after both of them and that teaches me how hard it really is to take care of another living thing they rely on my for food and love but at least my cat can hunt a mouse if she skips dinner the dog is completely dependent on people to feed it.

Without the punctuation, I have created a series of ideas strung together. Once this free write is done, I would go back and look for core ideas to write an essay about. Perhaps I really liked the idea about the dogs responding to people and how they are fun to play with. This then becomes the starting point for an essay.

4) Outlines

Outlines help put your brainstorms together into a cohesive unit. I recommend you do an outline *after* you brainstorm, since it requires you to have ideas to fill in the different sections. Some of you may be able to create an outline without brainstorming first, but I find most students put together their ideas in an organized manner by using the outline after they have brainstormed. An outline about pets might look like this:

I. First Paragraph—comparing my cat and dog
   A. Dogs
      1. Fun to play with
      2. Obedient
   B. Cats
      1. Independent
         a. does not need me for survival
         b. only want affection when he/she is ready
      2. Hunts for food
         a. mice
         b. birds

II. Second Paragraph—dogs make better pets
   A. playing in the park
      1. plays fetch with a stick
      2. wags tail when excited
      3. jumps when happy to see me
   B. Listens to my commands
      1. Sit
      2. Stay
      3. Rollover

One of the rules you need to know about an outline is this: whenever you have a Roman numeral I, you must also have a Roman numeral II. Whenever you have an A, you must also have a B. This is true for anything you insert into your outline. Each element of the outline is designed to tell yourself how you are going to organize the essay and what you are going to put in each paragraph. So, for example, in a five paragraph essay, you would have five Roman numerals. Within each Roman numeral, you may have several A, B, and Cs that might also have several other points that you need to expand using 1, 2, and 3. And you are not limited to using simple words like I did in my outline. Your outline can be as simple or complex as you need it to be. A good outline can be many pages and include sentences that you might actually use in your essay. The reason you should brainstorm first and then make an outline is that in order to fill in the outline, you must know what you are going to talk about. The outline is meant to help you go from the brainstorming process to the writing process.

CHAPTER 3 ACTIVITIES

Now, let us practice. The following list contains five words that I want you to brainstorm using whatever method you choose. On a separate piece of paper, brainstorm each word, and then write an outline of what you might want to write about.

1. Music

2. Sports

3. Food

4. Computers

5. Books

Brainstorm

_____

_____

_____

_____

_____

_____

_____

_____

_____

_____

_____

_____

_____

_____

_____

_____

_____

_____

CHAPTER 4

Creating a Thesis

Once you have a brainstorm and an outline, you are now ready to construct your argument. An argument is what you want to prove in your essay. It is the reason the essay exists. When you have narrowed down your topic for your essay, you want to assemble a core idea, some kind of foundation upon which you will build your essay. We call this element a **thesis.**

The first part of the thesis is called a **claim.** A claim is the essential, core element of an argument. It is what you believe—it is the position you are going to take in the essay. All claims can be broken down into three different types of opinions.

1) Claim of Value

A claim of value makes a judgment of some kind or expresses approval or disapproval. It often attempts to prove that some action, belief, or condition is right or wrong, good or bad. You will often see words like right and wrong, good and bad, better and worse. These are clues that you are writing a claim of value. Here are some examples:

"Foreign cars are better than American cars because of their resale value."

"Experimenting on animals is wrong."

"Laws that allow seeing-eye dogs into restaurants are a good thing."

2) Claim of Policy

A claim of policy argues that a law, rule, or policy needs to be changed. It argues that certain conditions should exist or some kind of solution should be adopted. When you use words like "should," "must," or "needs" you are often making a suggestion that a change needs to take place or something should be done to fix a problem. Here are some examples using the same concepts as in the claim of value:

"People should buy a foreign car instead of an American car."

"Experimenting on animals must be stopped in order to prevent cruel conditions for the animals."

"Restaurants should always allow seeing-eye dogs and other service animals into their business."

3) Claim of Fact

A claim of fact states that a condition has existed, currently exists, or will exist in the future. In addition, a claim of fact is something that can be proven, no matter if the claim ends up being true or false. For example, if I say, "The Los Angeles Angels of Anaheim will win the World Series in 2010," I have made a claim of fact. That claim can be proven in the future. Even if I am proven wrong, it is still considered a claim of fact because it is an opinion that can be supported with arguments. Words like *will* or *are* give you a clue that you are writing a claim of fact. Claims of fact often use statistical evidence inside the claim because it makes the claim provable. In the following examples, a test can be made to prove each of these claims. Even if the claim sounds like an opinion, it is still called a claim of fact.

"Foreign cars outsell American cars 2 to 1 because foreign cars are more reliable."

"Twenty percent of the animals used in laboratory experiments suffer in cruel conditions."

"Restaurants that allow seeing-eye dogs will see an increase in profit."

Notice how each of these sentences varies based on the kind of claim given. Each argument is slightly different, but they all can be categorized as one of these kinds of claims. Each one can be a thesis in an essay. You can still prove what it is you want to argue. Each sentence is still an opinion; the underlying principle in any argument.

Once you have established your claim as part of your thesis, you need the second element. You need to explain **"why"** your claim is important. This "why" can refer to many things. It can answer the question, "why am I writing about this?" It can also answer the question, "why should anybody care?" The "why" can even refer to bigger social issues in society, like "why is this important to society?" Based on your topic, the "why" element will change. It is up to you to determine how to approach your thesis in a way that will include what you are going to write about and why. Essentially, answering "why" gives your essay a reason to exist. The more focused and clearly you write your claim and the more purpose you give your thesis, the better your essay will turn out.

A thesis tells the reader exactly what you are going to write about in your essay. Think of it as a roadmap. I should be able to read your thesis and know what you believe and what you are attempting to prove. **A thesis can be several sentences!** Sometimes, complex ideas require many sentences, and when you start including the answers to "why" your claim is important, you will see your thesis develop. It will start to drive your essay.

The following examples were given in the first part of the chapter. They are the claims that make up the first part of the thesis. This time, the ideas answer the question why, making these examples a complete thesis. As you read, notice the type of claim being made and why it is important. Based on the thesis examples below, could you write an essay?

"Foreign cars are better than American cars because of their resale value. Understanding what attributes affect the resale value of a car will allow an individual to make the right choice when shopping for a new vehicle."

"Experimenting on animals must be stopped in order to prevent cruel conditions for the animals. These conditions set by laboratories conducting research deny the animals their rights. As a civilized society, we need to fight for animal rights since animals cannot stand up for themselves."

"Restaurants that allow seeing-eye dogs will see an increase in profit. Accepting animals that help people will also encourage those who rely on the animals to go to that restaurant, thus, resulting in an increase in sales. In addition, others will see this as a gesture of kindness, and restaurant owners will see an increase in patrons."

Many students have trouble formulating a thesis. This is why brainstorming is very important. A good thesis does not just "appear." You need to work on your ideas in order to figure out what you are going to write about. Sometimes, you need to investigate and research your topic before you write your position (research can often reveal things you did not know before, hence, changing your position).

Go back and look at the brainstorm about pets. There are many ideas there, and it would be difficult to write an essay about all of them. After further research, I decided to write about dogs. I discovered outside resources that explained in great detail how dogs are used as rescue animals and how dogs can be used to help the handicapped. I can even re-brainstorm those ideas to help develop my argument and use those ideas as support in the essay.

The trick to writing a good thesis is finding the universal theme that you are going to write about. Each paragraph in your essay will support this universal theme. The universal theme should be specific within the realm of the topic you are going to write about. So when you have created the list of things that you want to write about in your essay, you need to find the one thing they all have in common. What is it you are actually going to write about in your essay?

In my example, I found that there are many things to talk about in terms of the positive influences a dog can have. But instead of listing all of those things, I am simply going to make a blanket statement. For example, "Dogs are an integral part of our society." This statement is specific to my topic, but at the same time allows me to write about many different things, proving how dogs are an integral part of our society. I am not limited to a list. Instead, I have unlimited potential because I can write as many paragraphs as needed to prove my thesis. The "why" part will include how the dogs are integral parts of our society, and I want to show what they can do in our lives, so I might write something like this: "Dogs are an integral part of our society. Through their superior senses, dogs have proven to be a valuable asset in our lives." I could even add another sentence. I could make one more statement claiming that we need to keep dogs trained in all the different things we use them for. Therefore, I could also write: "Dogs are an integral part of our society. Through their superior senses, dogs have proven to be a valuable asset in our lives. We should keep dogs trained at all times." This would answer part of the "why."

Now that you see my thesis, you should be able to see how I might organize my essay. My goal is to prove several things. First I will discuss some of those superior senses. Then I will show how those senses help us in our lives. I will also need to show how a dog's life is integrated in our society. I will rely on some of my research mentioned earlier to prove this. Certainly, this essay would be more than five paragraphs. I would need to provide several examples and support throughout my essay in order to prove my claims.

You should also recognize the type of claim used in my thesis. Ultimately, I am arguing a claim of policy because I am suggesting that dogs should be trained at all times. Why? Because they are useful in search and rescue and they have the ability to help the handicapped.

But this is not the only thesis that can come out of this topic. I can re-work my thesis as I write my essay. Perhaps I realized that this thesis does not communicate my position clearly enough. I could go back and write the following: "Society needs to keep training programs for dogs used in social services. Because of a dog's superior senses and abilities, they are an integral part of our lives." Even though this thesis has one less sentence than before, it still clearly communicates what I am going to write about and why.

Remember, your thesis is not set in stone until you turn in your paper. Think of it as a ball of clay. You can mold it however you choose. For example, you finish your essay and you realize you have changed what it is you set out to prove. You can always go back and change a thesis to match what you wrote. Sometimes, in a very long essay, your thesis may not even be the first thing you write. You can always come back to it and make it reflect what it is you wrote about, learned about, and proved in the rest of your essay.

Now go back to your brainstorms from the previous chapter and write a thesis. You may need to go back to your original brainstorm to see some of the things that you might want to add if you are going to write a full essay. Remember, your thesis will be more than one sentence. You are going to need to answer the question "why?" For example, why is this topic important and why should it be discussed? Writing a good, strong thesis takes practice.

Finally, there are other tricks to help you understand what you believe and why. In the Appendix, you will find the "World View" activity to help you understand what you believe and why. As you do this activity, be sure to think about how this applies to topics you might have to write about in your class.

Additional Information: Writing a Thesis

1. A thesis consists of two or more sentences.
   A. The first sentence is the claim. This is your argument/opinion.
   B. The second sentence answers "why?" It is a reason your claim exists.
   C. To help answer the question "why," try starting your sentence with, "This is important because…"
2. Avoid using first person in your thesis. The reader knows it is your opinion.
3. A thesis is not a question; however, a thesis can answer a question.
4. A thesis cannot be a direct quote or a summary because those things are not your opinion. It is someone else's opinion.
5. A thesis should avoid a list of topics you are going to write about. It should be a specific argument you plan to prove in your essay using as many supporting paragraphs needed to prove the argument.
6. Avoid writing a "report" type thesis. This means a thesis needs to reflect your argument/belief, not what others are currently saying about your topic. Do not report the information about a topic—argue using the information you discovered doing research.
7. Remember, a thesis can change. Many students find that the thesis is different from what the essay proved. You can always go back and change the thesis to mirror what you discussed in the essay.

CHAPTER 4 ACTIVITIES

Here is the list again from the previous chapter to help you practice writing a thesis. Keep in mind what kind of claim you are writing. Giving it a label will help you know what you are arguing. For each topic, try writing three different thesis using the three different kinds of claims.

1. Music

2. Sports

3. Food

4. Computers

5. Books

Name: _____   Date: _____

Brainstorm

_____

_____

_____

_____

_____

_____

_____

_____

_____

_____

_____

_____

_____

_____

_____

_____

_____

Name: _____   Date: _____

Thesis

_____

_____

_____

_____

_____

_____

_____

_____

_____

_____

_____

_____

_____

_____

_____

_____

_____

_____

Name: _____   Date: _____

Support

_____

_____

_____

_____

_____

_____

_____

_____

_____

_____

_____

_____

_____

_____

_____

_____

_____

_____

PART 2

Paragraphs

CHAPTER 5

Introductions

Now that you have written a thesis, you need to put it somewhere. The thesis comes towards the beginning of your essay, usually in the **introductory paragraph.** The introductory paragraph is designed to inform the reader of your topic, your thesis, and to get the reader interested in examining your ideas. We often call the introduction your "hook" or "theme." It gets the reader interested in your topic and thesis so that they want to keep reading. A good "theme" can be used throughout your essay.

The thesis comes towards the end of the introductory paragraph. It should never be the first sentence because the thesis would be out of context. Without setting up your topic, the thesis would not serve any purpose by being the first sentences in your introduction. You want the sentences used in the introduction to lead smoothly into the thesis. The type of essay you are writing will help determine which method of introduction you should use. If you have more than one choice, choose the method that you are most comfortable with.

1) The Inverted Pyramid or Funnel Method

Using this method requires that you begin writing your introduction in general terms and move to a specific idea, where the specific idea is actually your thesis. Think of it as an upside-down triangle. Your sentences and ideas will be general ideas. With each sentence you will get more specific until you reach your thesis. The advantage of this method is that it is easy to use and can work for any essay type.

The following student sample, written by Ikeia Dawkins, demonstrates how to write an introduction using the funnel method by responding to the writing prompt "Should homeless people be forced off the streets?" Notice how the author moves from general ideas to more specific ideas before introducing the topic of the homeless.

65

When it comes to humanity, the hearts of men and women are open to compassion because it is a mutual topic shared by most people. Whenever there are issues involving healthcare, labor, or housing laws the attention of the public is passionately caught up in them. Most people desire food, clothing, and shelter. These yearnings are exactly what makes the human race work hard to obtain these necessities. However, there are those living in communities and throughout society that do not have these vital needs. These are the homeless men and women living in our streets. They are constantly feeling the pain and humiliation of being poor. The hardships they endure are especially difficult during the cold winter months. Fearing that they could be suffering in such conditions brings up a question on how society should act to deal with this problem. The question is this: should the police force the homeless into shelters in the cold winter months? Homeless people openly accept and refuse help and society understands both of these reactions. Society is faced with many controversial methods for helping those that are homeless and those that refuse assistance. Helping the homeless should always take precedence over any choice of the individual homeless person. In the harsh winter months, officials need to help the homeless in order to save lives.

2) Quotation Method

Using this method requires that you begin your essay with a quote. This quote can be from a textbook, a source, or a famous quote from the past. Usually, the quote is the first thing that appears in your introduction. The rest of the introduction connects the quote to your thesis, which will appear at the end of the introductory paragraph. The important thing here is that you have a good quotation to begin your paper. A good quote will encourage the reader to keep reading. Another advantage is that if you have a good quote, you can always reference it again throughout the essay.

The following student sample, written by Flor Espinosa, demonstrates how to write an introduction using the quotation method by responding to the writing prompt "Should women serve in the military?"

Harry Truman, the thirty-third president of the United States stated, ". . . I found that the men and women who got to the top were those who did the jobs they had in hand, with everything they had of energy and enthusiasm and hard work" ("Harry S. Truman Quotes and Quotations"). Throughout history women have played and accomplished many important roles in life. Some have become heads of nations or captains of industry, while others have become successful lawyers and great surgeons. However, the question remains whether women should play important roles in military combat. The fact of the matter is that women do not possess the physical strength, are at a high risk of being sexually abused, and can be the cause of disruption of combat unit operations if they were to fill active combat roles. Whereas Truman talked about a woman's abilities to accomplish anything through mental toughness, serving in the military requires a different kind of ability. Sometimes, there are things that can stop a woman from reaching the "top." Women should not be allowed to fight as front-line soldiers where combat is a requirement or be used in potentially hostile combat situations. The consequences can be detrimental to both the individuals in combat and to the morale of the military.

Works Cited

"Harry S. Truman Quotes and Quotations." *Famous Quotes and Authors.*

Famous Quotes and Authors.com, 2009. Web. 4 Apr. 2009.

3) Short Story Method

Using this method requires that you begin your essay with a brief story that connects some ideas to your thesis. The short story can be a retelling of history, the discussion of current events, or something fictional that relates to your topic. The advantage of using the short story method is that you can really hook the reader and get them interested in your essay. It is also a good way to connect your topic to a larger social issue. Remember, your essay should not include personal statements, so your short story method cannot include a story about yourself.

The following student sample, written by Franklin Chandler, demonstrates how to write an introduction using a short story to hook the reader. The topic for this paragraph was "gun control." By using the word *imagine* to start the paragraph Franklin has already put the reader into the mindset needed to make the reader "feel" the topic. Also, you should notice that there seems to be several different kinds of claims. What kind of claim do you think Franklin is making?

Imagine ending a hard day's work by closing up your store for the night. As you walk to your car, you feel you are alone in the parking lot—you were the last to leave, so there are no other cars around you. Suddenly, two men approach, their hands in their pockets. You freeze, uncertain of what the men want. One of the men pulls a gun out of his pocket, points it at you, and asks for your money. You have just been robbed. It is stories like this that are happening on a regular basis. People are using guns to commit crimes. Gun control laws need to be stricter and enforced throughout the country. People should be allowed to walk alone at night and not feel afraid. Using modern technologies, many gun control laws will keep guns away from criminals. With stricter gun control laws, society will be a safer place.

4) Question Method

Using this method requires that you begin your essay with a series of questions. Of course, if you choose the right questions, your thesis should be the answer. Some students have a problem with this method because it does not make their introductory paragraph long enough. A student would have to make up three to four questions, plus their thesis, to make the paragraph long enough. The advantage to this method is that it is easily combined with any other method. For example, you can start with a question, tell a short story that answers the question, and then give your thesis.

The following student sample, written by Melody McCormick, demonstrates how to write an introduction using the question method by responding to the writing prompt "Discuss the theories that argue that Edgar Allan Poe was 'racist.'"

Is Edgar Allan Poe a racist? Or do his works simply reflect the attitudes of his times? He has been described as many things: genius, artist, passionate, tormented and even racist. There is no doubt that his body of work is veiled in multiple levels of controversy. The different schools of thought and approach to this subject include decades of discussion and debate. The novel *The Narrative of Arthur Gordon Pym of Nantucket* seems to be the focal point of recent discussion about Poe and racism. The search for the true "character" of Poe begins with understanding the events of one Arthur Gordon Pym, the main character of Poe's hotly debated novel. There are many critics who argue that behind Pym's narrative lies the heart of a racist. If Poe's work should be read as such, this opens his writing to a totally racial interpretation. Most critics have likened Poe to a hard-boiled racist; his need to classify the blacks as separate and lesser than the whites is the foundation for their racial theories. However, this may not be the case, because reading Poe as a racist limits our understanding of Poe and his characters. Poe was actually writing what he knew and with a specific purpose, for an audience he knew would read his book and in a time which accepted the racial implications in his story.

5) Definition Method

Using this method requires that you begin your essay by defining an important idea or word that is unique to your essay. It is common to begin with a dictionary definition, then proceed to offer an extended definition (see Chapter 9). For example, if your essay is about some important social issue, such as racism, you can begin your essay with defining the term *racism* from the dictionary. Then, you can proceed to offer a new or extended definition. This would become the main argument of your essay.

The following student sample, written by Flor Espinosa, demonstrates how to write an introduction using the definition method by responding to the writing prompt "Define what it means to be a 'leader.'"

The *American Heritage Dictionary* defines a leader as someone who "guides or conducts" ("Leader"). But the extended definition of a leader is someone who is an example to his people, a person who has authority and someone who guides his group properly within certain boundaries. It can be a group, a team, a state, a home or a nation. However, the best way to demonstrate what it means to be a leader is to use an example. In the Old Testament in the Bible, Moses was one who embodied these characteristics. Like a true leader, Moses' pattern, authority and guidance only benefited his people by directing and instructing them on how to survive. By understanding Moses and his leadership abilities, we will see how the definition applies to an individual. Once established, these attributes will benefit those who strive to be leaders today, which will allow individuals to be the best kind of leader in society.

Works Cited

"Leader." *American Heritage Dictionary*. 4th ed. 2001. Print.

6) Startling Statistic Method

When doing research, you may come across a surprising piece of information about your topic. Often, these statistics or data that affect you will also affect your reader. A good way to start your introduction would be to use that startling statistic in order to grab your reader's attention. Once you introduce the information, you then elaborate and connect it to your thesis.

The following student sample, written by Alina Salazar, demonstrates how to write an introduction using the startling statistic method by responding to the writing prompt "Abortion."

Throughout the world there are 137 babies aborted every hour, which comes down to 1 baby being aborted every 26 seconds ("Minnesota Citizens Concerned for Life"). With this many potential lives being destroyed, it really makes a person wonder whether abortion is an ethical decision. Arguments on whether abortions are moral or immoral have been around for decades and continue today. Abortion is a very controversial issue and every person has their own views on whether they support pro-life or pro-choice. For every point each side brings, the opposing side will find an equal but opposite reason for that belief. In essence, an individual's belief affects how they support the pro-life and pro-choice debate. Understanding the two sides of the argument will help us understand why the argument exists and how solutions through compromise might exist in the future.

Works Cited

"Minnesota Citizens Concerned for Life." *Minnesota Citizens Concerned for Life.* Minnesota Citizens Concerned for Life, 2009. Web. 1 Jan. 2009.

7) The Survey Method

Using this method requires that you begin your essay by basically stating everything you are going to write about. This method is usually reserved for very large papers where your thesis is your entire introductory paragraph. When you do research for the final project and you come across journals, you may see the survey method used in those journals. In essence, your topic is so big that you need many sentences to explain what it is you are going to write about and why. Though you may not use this method on one of your normal essays, some of you may consider this method for term papers or final research papers.

The following student sample, written by Dominic Delano, demonstrates how to write an introduction using the survey method by responding to the writing prompt "Discuss Anne Bradstreet's poetry in early American literature."

Anne Bradstreet, often regarded as one of the earliest American poets, played an important role in defining the culture of the New World. Her poetry and prose described what life was like in early America, focusing on what it meant to be a woman, mother and wife in a Puritan society. Her importance in literature is great—from exploring the new frontier to writing of the human experience, Anne Bradstreet was very influential. The study of her work continues today; critics argue whether or not her work fits into the Puritan religion and philosophy. It can be argued that Anne Bradstreet's poetry and prose transcends the Puritan religion. First, there is a difference between Bradstreet the Puritan and Bradstreet the poet. As a Puritan, she was a devoted wife, good mother and very hard worker. As a poet, she was able to articulate her problems with the Puritan life style. By studying her work, it is clear that some of her poetry and prose rebel against the Puritan doctrine. By experimenting with poetry, Bradstreet was able to convey her personal feelings of living in a new land, describing her mental state and her relationship to her husband, children, neighbors and even God. First, we will begin with a brief accounting of Bradstreet's life followed by a discussion of the concepts that make up the Puritan religion. Then, a discussion of the arguments about why Bradstreet's work is considered Puritan will occur. Finally, it will be proven that Bradstreet's poetry should be considered as more than just a Puritan writing. She takes the time to describe the world around her and deal with issues many people must have faced, doing so as an educated woman within a Puritan world.

There are many things to consider in this chapter. Writing a good introduction takes practice. Here are a few other tips to help you write a strong introductory paragraph:

1. You can combine different methods to create your own introductory paragraph. Remember, if you are trying to get a reader's attention, combining the methods presented here might make a creative and successful introduction.
2. A question can never be a thesis. You can ask a question that leads to your thesis, but the thesis cannot be a question.
3. A thesis cannot be a quote by someone else. Remember, it is your argument.
4. By definition, a paragraph is five or more sentences, so your introduction will be at least five or more sentences.

CHAPTER 5 ACTIVITIES

Since you have a thesis written from the previous chapter, go ahead and make an introductory paragraph with that thesis. Or, you can try a new topic from the list below.

1. Music

2. Sports

3. Food

4. Computers

5. Books

6. Life on a college campus

7. Why reading books helps you write

8. Video Games

Name: _____   Date: _____

Brainstorm

_____

_____

_____

_____

_____

_____

_____

_____

_____

_____

_____

_____

_____

_____

_____

_____

_____

_____

_____

Name: _____   Date: _____

Introduction

_____

_____

_____

_____

_____

_____

_____

_____

_____

_____

_____

_____

_____

_____

_____

_____

_____

_____

CHAPTER 6

Developing Supporting Paragraphs

Now that you have developed a thesis and put it in your introduction, it is time to learn how to write the rest of the essay. An essay consists of supporting paragraphs (aka body paragraphs) that aim to prove your thesis. Since these kinds of paragraphs make up the bulk of your essay, they are extremely important.

Every supporting paragraph in your essay serves a purpose. It is designed to prove your thesis. Remember, you claimed something or offered an argument when you wrote a thesis—you use the rest of the essay to prove that thesis.

This means that all supporting paragraphs are interconnected. Although these supporting paragraphs contain different ideas, all of the ideas connect back to the thesis. If you do this correctly, the essay will flow.

You can think of these paragraphs as extended arguments. You take one idea, expand it in your own words, and then prove it. If you break things down this way, writing any kind of essay will be easier. And sometimes, it might be easier to start writing a supporting paragraph before writing the introduction.

Students always wonder: "Where do I put support, like outside sources?" For example, during your research, you found a great piece of evidence that you want to use to prove your thesis. This is exactly what you want (and the reason you should work on developing good research skills). Most students put this evidence in one of two places—at the beginning of the paragraph or at the end of the paragraph. Actually, neither place is a "good" place to put your evidence. In general, you want the first sentence to introduce the paragraph, so if the evidence comes first, it will not be set into the context of what you are proving. And in general, you do not want to end the paragraph with this evidence because you always want a chance to explain it and connect it to your thesis. In other words, do not drop a quote and run!

Here is a quick list to help you remember how to assemble a supporting paragraph. I will explain each element, but the goal is to help you remember how to write strong supporting paragraphs.

T/S = *Topic Sentence*
EL = *El*aborate argument
E/Q = *Example* or *Quote* for support
A = *Analyze* the example or quote
C/T = *Concluding* sentence or *Transition* sentence

I want to emphasize that each element in this mnemonic device (TSELEQACT) is not a sentence, but several sentences (or however many sentences needed for an explanation). If you make everything in the equation one sentence, your essay would be very rigid and structured. The goal is to make it flow.

Now, look at how these five elements break down.

1) *Topic Sentence*

The goal of a topic sentence within a supporting paragraph is to tell the reader what the paragraph is about. It is not that much different than a thesis—the thesis tells the reader what you are going to argue in the essay (using several sentences) and the topic sentence tells the reader what you are going to discuss in the paragraph (usually one sentence, but it can be more). In order to write a good topic sentence, go back and look at your thesis. Pull out ideas or things you want to prove (you can even go back and look at your brainstorm—see, everything is connected). Then, formulate the sentence, and create a single idea that this supporting paragraph will be about. It might look like a thesis statement with a focus on a specific idea.

2) *Elaborate Argument*

Now that you have a topic sentence, you need to elaborate *your* argument. This is where you explain yourself using sentences that communicate your ideas. What are you arguing? What are you trying to prove? Clarify! Explain! Elaborate! Remember, this is not one sentence. Typically, a good explanation takes several sentences. You want the reader to really understand your argument and what you have to say.

3) *Example or Quote*

Once you have made your argument clear, you want to look to really prove your argument by adding outside support. Outside support is anything that comes from someone or somewhere other than you. Look back at Chapter 1, where we discussed the different kinds of support. When doing research, you are going to encounter different types of support you want to use in your essay. This is the place in the paragraph where you put all that hard work to a good use. You want that support or example to prove your argument. For example, if you are arguing that dogs are an integral part of our society, you should be using support that proves that statement. If you find a quote by an animal expert, put it here. If you found an article and you summarize the main idea about how important dogs are, put it here. If you need help, go back to Chapter 1 to learn how to do research and Chapter 2 to learn how to format a quote correctly.

4) **Analyze**

Many students stop at the third part of the paragraph (E/Q). However, in order to write a strong supporting paragraph, you want to analyze your support. What does the quote mean? What do the statistics mean? How does this support connect to your argument? In this section of the paragraph, you want to take the time to tell the reader exactly what the support is designed to do. You need to explain the quote (if it is a difficult quote to understand) and show why it is helping your argument. Again, this usually takes a few sentences—it is quite possible you will need many sentences if you need to explain a complicated quote or complex idea. This analysis and explanation will not only connect back to your topic sentence, but it will also connect to your thesis.

5) **Conclude or *Transition***

When you are done presenting your argument using these methods, you want to find a way to end the paragraph. There are two options here because it depends on what comes after the supporting paragraph you are writing. When you offer a concluding sentence, you are ending the idea presented in the paragraph. This means you would begin a new idea in the next paragraph. If you transition, you are telling the reader that there is more to come—the next paragraph might continue the argument but still be related to the previous paragraph. Transitions are very important because they help the reader see the logical connections within the supporting paragraphs.

Here are a few other tips:

1. Although you see a pattern here, you do not have to use only one quote in a paragraph. You can add more quotes if you want. The goal of this "quick list" is to help you design and write a paragraph. What matters is the connection between the support and how you analyze it. So if you want another quote or more support, just be sure to analyze it. Your pattern might look like this:

T/S
EL
E/Q
A
E/Q
A
C

That would be great! If you could do this, you will create a very strong argument for your essay.

2. Take your time to explain yourself. Many students think that the elaboration that comes after the topic sentence is one sentence. It can be many sentences. The same is true for the analysis of the support. Take the time to explain yourself and connect your ideas. Expand! Expand! Expand! You will see a big difference in your writing.

3. There are many kinds of transition phrases to help you move between paragraphs. These transitions are not limited to your last sentence. They can also start the topic sentence in the next paragraph. Here is a list of several popular transitional phrases:

Addition:
also, again, furthermore, in addition, likewise, moreover, similarly
Consequence:
accordingly, as a result, consequently, for this reason, hence, otherwise, therefore, thus
Exemplifying:
especially, for instance, in particular, namely, particularly, specifically, such as
Illustration:
for example, for instance, as an illustration, in this case

Emphasis:
above all, chiefly, with attention to, especially, particularly
Similarity:
comparatively, likewise, similar, moreover
Contrast and Comparison:
by contrast, conversely, instead, likewise, on one hand, on the other hand, on the contrary, rather, similarly, yet, but, however, still, nevertheless, in contrast
Exception:
aside from, besides, except, excluding, other than, outside of
Restatement:
in essence, in other words, namely, that is, that is to say, in short, in brief

The following student sample, written by Flor Espinosa, demonstrates how to write a supporting paragraph using the methods in this chapter. This paragraph is from an essay in response to the writing prompt "Should women serve in the military?" You also read the introduction to the essay as well. Notice how having a good, reliable outside source makes the paragraph stronger.

Men's instinctive nature to protect a woman can cause the disruption of a combat unit's operation and execution of orders. Therefore, women should not be allowed to fight in the battlefield. The efficiency of military operations would be put in danger if male soldiers go beyond appropriate tactics in order to defend a woman. This situation would worsen if there is a romantic relationship between male and female soldiers in combat. This can potentially disrupt combat and put people's lives at risk. Lt. Col. Dave Grossman mentioned that female soldiers in the Israel Defense Forces have been officially banned from performing close combat operations. He states, "The cause for removing women from front-line operations was due to the enraged male soldiers after witnessing a wounded woman." The Israel Defense Forces saw a complete loss of control over soldiers who apparently experienced a protective, violent behavior which could have resulted in a failed mission and massacre of the enemy leading to the loss of many lives.

Works Cited

Grossman, Dave. *On Killing: The Psychological Cost of Learning to Kill in War and Society.* New York: Back Bay Books, 1996. Print.

The following student sample, written by Morris Thompson, demonstrates how to write a complex supporting paragraph using the methods in this chapter. This paragraph is from an essay in response to the prompt "Define the Hemingway Hero." Notice how this paragraph includes two quotes and the analysis needed to connect the quotes.

Hemingway's fiction is full of male characters who exhibit masculine qualities. Many of his characters play sports or have a deep and vast knowledge of a sport. The fact that they all have sports in common is an important characteristic for what is known as "The Hemingway Hero." Stewart Rodnon writes, ". . . Hemingway obviously considers that the virtues which are fundamental for sports are the same as those needed to face life" (88). Virtues, such as honor, courage, patience, practice, and following a strong code, or ethic, become applicable in more than just the sports world. These traits are valued in everyday life. There is an overlap between the definition of the male character, the sports they play, and how they live life. The Hemingway Hero is a male character that follows a strict code. This code dictates the actions and choices the character must make. The character respects the natural world and they are aware of their surroundings and environments. The male character typically exhibits a certain level of masculinity by demonstrating all of these traits. For Hemingway, it is not about the number of trophies won or how big the prize is, but how someone prepares and practices that makes the difference. For example, Hemingway loved fishing. Jack Hemingway, Ernest's oldest son, states in the foreword in the book *Hemingway on Fishing,* "In our family not only fly fishing but all sporting forms of fishing were a sort of religion" (Hemingway *xi*). He was more interested in the art of fishing, how one puts a lure on a hook and casts it in the water, about the art of patience when waiting to catch a fish, than the number of fish caught. In Hemingway's world, it is how you do everything that is important in defining of the masculine sports hero.

Works Cited

Hemingway, Ernest. *Hemingway on Fishing.* Ed. Nick Lyons. New York:

    Lyons Press, 2000. Print.

Rodnon, Stewart. *Sports, Sporting Codes, and Sportsmanship in the Work of*

    Ring Lardner, James T. Farrell, Ernest Hemingway and William

    Faulkner. Diss. New York University, 1961. Ann Arbor: University

    Microfilms, Inc., 1972. Print.

CHAPTER 6 ACTIVITIES

Now it is time to practice. You can take any topic found in the book so far and write a well-developed supporting paragraph using the techniques in this chapter. Or, here is a list of some new topics:

1. Music

2. Sports

3. Food

4. Computers

5. Books

6. Life on a college campus

7. Why reading books helps you write

8. Video Games

9. Vacations

10. Hobbies

11. Pets

Name: _____   Date: _____

Brainstorm

_____

_____

_____

_____

_____

_____

_____

_____

_____

_____

_____

_____

_____

_____

_____

_____

_____

_____

_____

Name: _____   Date: _____

Thesis

_____

_____

_____

_____

_____

_____

_____

_____

_____

_____

_____

_____

_____

_____

_____

_____

_____

_____

94

Name: _____ Date: _____

Support

_____

_____

_____

_____

_____

_____

_____

_____

_____

_____

_____

_____

_____

_____

_____

_____

_____

_____

_____

_____

_____

CHAPTER 7

Conclusions

There is one more kind of paragraph. It comes at the very end of the essay. We call this a **concluding paragraph**. A good conclusion should fit with the introduction. In other words, the conclusion should tie together what you have argued throughout the essay. Just as the introduction hooked the reader, the conclusion ends the hook. The conclusion finalizes the essay, drawing it to a close. Based on what method you used to start your paper, it will have a great influence on how you end your essay.

One of the easiest ways to construct a conclusion is to take the following steps. First, you need to rewrite your thesis in such a way that you keep the meaning but use different words. After all, your thesis appears on page one and your conclusion will come many pages later. It is a good idea to restate the thesis so that the reader knows everything you have proved thus far has been validated. Once you have rewritten your thesis, go back and look at each supporting paragraph. Can you summarize these paragraphs in one sentence? If you can (and you may need to do so in more than one sentence), each of those one sentence summaries will go into your conclusion in the same order they appear in your essay. In essence, your conclusion will be created by using a sentence summarizing each supporting paragraph in the essay. This is one of the easiest ways to construct a conclusion.

Your conclusion is a paragraph too, so it must have at least five or more sentences. Many students end their paper with a conclusion that has less than five sentences, which is something you want to avoid.

At this point, it is usually a good idea to add a sentence or two that connects with your overall theme that you established in your introductory paragraph. For example, if you use a quote in the introductory paragraph, then you can bring up that quote again at the end of your paper. Another example can be if you found a theme or a hook in the introduction and throughout the essay, then you can refer back to that at the end of your conclusion. Remember, the goal of your conclusion is to summarize what you have stated and to conclude ideas and themes in a coherent manner.

Here are some rules about writing conclusions:

1. You cannot introduce any new ideas or any new evidence in your conclusion. It is the ending summary, not a place to discuss new topics. If you find yourself adding something new to your conclusion, then make that idea a new paragraph and build your conclusion later. So remember, "nothing new!"

2. You are allowed to end your conclusion with a question as long as the answer is the essay itself. Many students ask a question in their conclusion. However, the answer is something different than what they argued in their essay. You want to avoid doing this.

3. The conclusion is a place to draw upon some emotion in your reader if you are writing an essay of that nature. For example, in a persuasive essay in which you are trying to convince the reader to take action, you could demonstrate the consequences of those actions by appealing to the reader's emotions.

4. It is a good strategy to use some of the same techniques you used in the introduction. However, the trick is not to sound repetitive. That is why you want to summarize things in different words. But if you create a strong introduction that grabs your reader, do not be afraid to use the same technique again.

5. The conclusion is just as important as any part of your essay. After all, it is the last thing the reader will remember when they finish your essay. So make it a good ending!

The following student sample, written by Andrew Modugno, demonstrates how to write a conclusion by responding to the writing prompt "Should smoking cigarettes be banned?" Notice that even without the rest of the essay (all you see here is the last paragraph), you will get the sense of how the essay was organized and what topics were discussed in order to prove the thesis.

Public smoking does affect our society today. Not only does smoking affect the smoker, but many other things as well. Smoking affects our environment by polluting the air we breathe. It affects the worldwide littering problem, because cigarette butts are the most littered item in the world. In addition, countless fires have been started because of discarded cigarette butts. This happens both in the individual's home and in the wilderness, causing intense forest fires. Finally, thousands of innocent non-smokers die from second hand smoke and millions are affected daily. Yes, smoking is an addiction, but it is also a choice. This choice can have such a negative affect on so many people, animals, and the well being of our planet. This proves that cigarettes are bad not just for the smoker, but for everyone.

The following student sample, written by Evelyn Sandoval, demonstrates how to write a conclusion by responding to the writing prompt "Discuss some of the causes and effects of obesity." Notice that even without the rest of the essay (all you see here is the last paragraph), you will get the sense of how the essay was organized and what topics were discussed in order to prove the thesis.

In conclusion, people should choose their foods wisely. Too much fat in the body can lead to severe complications later on in people's lives. The most common effect of eating foods high in fat is obesity, and from there, heart diseases. People can also get high blood pressure, high cholesterol, insomnia, acne, and other types of health problems (all of which should be treated as serious). Many people all over the world have died because of all these effects saturated fats can have in the body. Children are being more affected today by not eating healthy. Starting at an early age, parents need to teach their children good eating habits and make them avoid foods high in fat.

Children should learn to enjoy eating fruits and vegetables. Combine this with physical activity; children will practice good, healthy habits for the rest of their lives. If everyone did this, the rates of obesity will quickly drop and people can have a longer and healthier life.

CHAPTER 7 ACTIVITIES

Take any work you have done and write a conclusion. If you have been doing the activities, then you should have an introduction, thesis, and supporting paragraph. Even without writing the rest of the essay, you can still write a conclusion. What would you conclude for your topic?

Name: _____   Date: _____

Brainstorm

_____

_____

_____

_____

_____

_____

_____

_____

_____

_____

_____

_____

_____

_____

_____

_____

_____

104

Name: _____   Date: _____

Thesis

_____

_____

_____

_____

_____

_____

_____

_____

_____

_____

_____

_____

_____

_____

_____

_____

_____

_____

Name: _____   Date: _____

Conclusion

_____

_____

_____

_____

_____

_____

_____

_____

_____

_____

_____

_____

_____

_____

_____

_____

_____

_____

PART 3

Essay Types

CHAPTER 8

The Process-Analysis Essay

Imagine walking down the street when a stranger stops you and asks for directions. If you are familiar with the location, you begin to develop a mental picture that maps the route from where you are standing to where the stranger needs to be. Within this mental map, you begin to see left and right turns and landmarks indicating where to go. Once you have the directions set in your head, you tell the stranger how to get to the location. You clearly explain where to turn and what to look for.

Every time you give directions like this, you are describing a *process*. A process is a set of directions (of any kind) that instructs an individual how to do something. For example, this includes location directions, building instructions, or even cooking instructions, like following a recipe in a cookbook. In other words, a process essay gives the reader directions or instructions about how to complete a task, or it tells how something is done. It explains the steps necessary, in chronological order, or gives information about the subject so that the reader knows the process involved.

There are two kinds of process essays: **instructional and informational.**

Instructional essays, as stated, are designed to teach the reader exactly the steps needed to complete a task. Essentially, you would write an essay explaining all the necessary steps to complete this task.

It is important to be thorough when writing this kind of essay. Think about how you make a peanut butter and jelly sandwich. As it turns out, this makes a good strategy for writing this kind of essay. Pretend a professor puts all the ingredients needed to make a peanut butter and jelly sandwich on the table, and then asks the class to give explicit instructions to make the sandwich. Students laugh because they think this is easy. For example, one student might shout, "Put the peanut butter on the bread!" The professor picks up the jar of peanut butter and puts it on the bread still inside the bag. Did the professor follow instructions? Were the instructions unclear, or were they missing a step? Hopefully, you understand that you need to twist the lid off of the jar first. You would also want to make sure to take the bread out of the bag as well. Being explicit in making a peanut butter and jelly sandwich is harder than it appears.

The point of this exercise is that we take instructions for granted. We know how to do things—you have probably made many peanut butter and jelly sandwiches in your lifetime. But have you ever had to teach someone else to make one? You know it is easy, but is it easy to explain?

When writing an instructional process essay, you have to be specific, including all the steps and tools needed to successfully perform the task. Do not take anything for granted. An essay like this is very structured—in other words, you will naturally organize the essay in the order needed to explain the process. For example, if you were writing an essay on the best way to fix a flat tire, you would need to start with the first step; gather the tools needed to perform the job, then start explaining the steps.

Informational essays do not necessarily have steps that must be followed in a precise order, but they still need to explain how something works. Whereas the instructional essay explains how to do something, the informational essay tells the reader why it works. You can think of this essay like a textbook—when you take a physics class, your textbook is informing you of how physics works.

Informational process essays usually teach the reader something new. It is very important to make sure your information is accurate. Research becomes extremely important in an essay like this. For example, in an informational essay explaining how a volcano is created and erupts, I would want to get the best resources available so that I can show the reader exactly what happens in volcanoes.

The process-analysis essay is what I call a "foundation essay." Throughout your academic career, you probably will not write too many process essays. However, the process essay is very important because it is something you may use in another kind of essay. So, when you practice writing a process essay, think about how you will use the process essay inside the paragraphs of a much larger essay. You often need to describe something to the reader within the essay you are writing. Whether it be analyzing literature or defending an argument, you will find yourself using the process-analysis essay method as a foundation in other types of essays.

Here are some additional tips for writing process-analysis essays and paragraphs.

1. If the process you are describing requires tools, parts, or materials, it is a good idea to talk about those things first. For example, if you are talking about a recipe and you need a specific utensil, it is better to describe what you need before you get to the point in the essay where you actually need to describe using it.

2. Use the number of steps in the process to help you decide on the number of paragraphs you will need in the body. Steps that are very small can be put together so that the paper is not too choppy.

3. Use a variety of transitions to show a progression of thought as you describe the process. For example, "The first thing you do is . . . The second area of interest. . . . The third way to prepare . . . "
4. Include examples or anecdotes to make your paper clearer and easier to follow, especially if one of the steps is confusing or difficult to explain. In other words, if you are explaining an overly complex procedure, maybe you explain it using a metaphor or analogy (see Chapter 13: Literary Analysis), something else the reader might understand so that they learn about the complex procedure you are explaining.
5. When you are done writing your process-analysis essay, go back and reread it. Does it make sense? Can you follow the instructions? If you give it to your friend, can they follow the process? This should be part of your proofreading process.

CHAPTER 8 ACTIVITIES

Now, it is time to practice the process-analysis essay. Below are some topics to get you started brainstorming. Remember to be specific in your explanation. And remember to see how writing this kind of essay will help you write paragraphs in other kinds of essays. For the instructional-based questions, do not be afraid to look up information—the more you learn about the topic before you write, the better you will be able to explain the process. Here are some possible process essay topics to write about:

1. How to juggle work and school.

2. How to make your favorite food.

3. How to prepare for a vacation.

4. What causes weather?

5. How does an internal combustion engine work?

6. What goes into making a movie/record/tv show/video game?

Name: _____   Date: _____

Brainstorm

_____

_____

_____

_____

_____

_____

_____

_____

_____

_____

_____

_____

_____

_____

_____

_____

_____

_____

_____

Name: _____   Date: _____

Thesis

_____

_____

_____

_____

_____

_____

_____

_____

_____

_____

_____

_____

_____

_____

_____

_____

_____

_____

Name: _____   Date: _____

Support

_____

_____

_____

_____

_____

_____

_____

_____

_____

_____

_____

_____

_____

_____

_____

_____

_____

The following student sample, written by Flor Espinosa, is a response to the writing prompt, "How to Juggle Work and School" (number 1 from the list provided). Notice how the student uses a step-by-step process, clearly labeled at the beginning of the supporting paragraphs. Also, as you read, be sure to think about the steps as being something you could do. Do you see what kind of process-analysis essay this can be labeled? Finally, notice how this essay is based on experience and does not use any outside sources. If you were to write this essay, what could you research to help support the argument?

Espinosa 1

Flor Espinosa

English 101

05-26-07

How to Juggle Work and School

Many people struggle every day to achieve their goals and accomplish their tasks. Some struggle to go to school while others struggle to work at home raising children. Doing both things at the same time is not an easy job. A mother of two small children who works full time at home has no choice but to learn how to juggle work and school. Doing both is the key to success at both things. Working with your spouse, scheduling your time wisely, and limiting your entertainment are steps born out of personal experience that can help you manage work at home and school at the same time. If these techniques are mastered, the individual might be rewarded with good grades and a happy home and the possibility of success in the future.

Espinosa 2

First, an individual needs to learn how to work together with his/her spouse. It is very important to have the spouse's cooperation and blessing before starting school. Otherwise, going to school will only end up in arguments and frustrations. At first, talk to the spouse about the desire to go to school and how much support is needed to achieve the goals. Tell him/her all of the benefits it will bring if you were to get a degree, not only for you, but also for the family. Also, discuss the sacrifice involved for both of you as well as for the kids. Once he/she supports the idea of you going to school, come to an agreement with him/her where he/she can be available to take care of the kids after work or on certain nights or weekends, depending on the kind of job he/she has. After you know your spouse's availability, which most likely is on nights and weekends, go ahead and register for classes for the semester during those times. If you choose a class during the time when no one is home to watch the kids, you will be distracted and not learn from going to class. Many schools and colleges have evening and night classes, specifically designed to help those people who are trying to go to school and raise a family.

Second, learning to schedule your time wisely is very important. At first, it helps to write down a weekly schedule where you set aside specific days to do different things. For example, set aside Monday, Wednesday night and Saturday morning for classes and Tuesday, Thursday, and Saturday night set aside to study or do homework. Sometimes, you may have to sacrifice some sleep during midterms, finals, or deadlines. Knowing that this is a natural thing that will happen is important in balancing time. Try to avoid scheduling several late nights in a row. This will help you recover by having days in which going to bed early helps the body heal. In addition, be realistic in choosing the number of classes. It is better not to take more classes than you can handle in the beginning as you gradually adjust to going to school. Fewer classes might mean it takes longer to graduate, but you will be thankful for this when you are conflicted on how to spend your time during the week.

Along with your weekly schedule, write a daily home routine. In other words, you should know what you and your family are doing throughout the day. This will really help you stay organized and balance your schedule. For example, from the moment you wake up, be diligent and work at a good pace. Schedule a time for breakfast followed by a bath for yourself and the kids. This works really well because it saves you a lot of time. Making a visual chart for you and your family will help everyone stay focused throughout the day. After breakfast, you can set aside a couple of hours in the morning to spend time with your kids. You can go for a stroll, play with them at the park, drive to the library, or visit a friend that has small children too. Around mid-day, come back home and feed them their lunch. Then you can establish a nap

Espinosa 4

time for the kids. Take advantage of this time to do some school homework or studying because you need the "quiet time" to be able to concentrate. Once your kids wake up, try to learn to work with them to get practical things done at home such as getting dinner ready, doing laundry, going grocery shopping, cleaning the house, etc. Establishing a daily schedule seems quite challenging but not impossible. It is worth it because it will allow you to have the night free to study or go to school. After all, the goal is to take care of the family and go to school, so having a planned schedule, both for the entire week and throughout the day, is very important.

Finally, choosing home and school means that you might have to learn to limit your entertainment. If you are serious about what you want to achieve, you have to prioritize your recreation. You will realize that it is important to have some vacations (short or long) with your family during the semester. You can schedule these times during spring break or holidays between the semesters. You can visit some relatives, go up to the mountains or spend the weekend at a local town. After that, you can also schedule a weekly time to be with them. For example, you can go on Sunday to church meetings or social times for the family at a park, and then in the afternoon you can go out to lunch or dinner or just spend time together at home. Going window shopping, watching television, partying or socializing for a long time may not be such a good idea while you are going to school. For example, if you are an active member of a church or organization and participate in many meetings, you may have to cut back on your amount of time there. Understanding the fine balance between recreation and entertainment and the time needed to attend school is very important. Taking time for a vacation can be important, but understanding the balance between the time away from school and the consequence of missing your studies is just as important.

In conclusion, juggling life between working at home with small children and going to school can be manageable by using many different methods. Working together with your spouse, scheduling your time wisely and limiting your entertainment are all steps you can take to be effective in school. Following the steps here is only the beginning. Once you find what works for you, go with it and make a life that supports both your schooling and your life at home. Both things can be accomplished, even though it may seem impossible for busy people who stay at home with a family and have a desire to go to school. Following the tips presented here should make the decision to do both a little bit easier.

CHAPTER 9

The Definition Essay

I know you have heard this before—if you come across a word and you do not know the meaning, look it up in a dictionary. But how many students actually do this?

Here is a word for you: *legerdemain.*
Sentence: "John's reputation for legerdemain left him with few friends."

If you saw this sentence, would you stop and look it up? Once you discover the word's meaning, you will begin to see why the definition essay is so important. What does this word mean in the context of the sentence?

Like the process-analysis essay, the **definition essay** is important both as a stand-alone essay and as paragraphs within a bigger assignment. The definition essay focuses on words, terms, and concepts as a means of communicating a definition. The definition essay is still an argument—essentially, you are arguing the definition of a word.

The definition essay draws not only on the dictionary definition of a word, but also on an **extended definition.** A dictionary usually offers a direct definition of a word (the common usage) and includes the part of speech and the etymology of the word. However, within that context, there are varying degrees of what a word means, and certainly some words have multiple definitions. This is called *denotation* (the specific meaning of a word) and *connotation* (the implied meaning of a word). For example, a "snake" is defined as a legless, scaled, cold-blooded reptile. That is the denotation of the word *snake.* However, if you call someone a "snake," insulting them for a cruel act, you are using the connotation of the word. Chances are, if you are asked to write an essay about the word *snake,* you would develop that essay based on the word's connotation.

The definition essay usually begins with some sort of formal definition. However, it *extends* or develops the formal definition to include varying aspects of the subject, including social and colloquial meanings. A definition essay may also build on the various meanings as dictated by a society. Your job is to argue that extended definition. For example, you can find the word *food* in the dictionary and put that definition towards the beginning of the essay. Then, you can argue an extended definition of the word. You could easily approach the definition of food from a psychological, cultural, or historical aspect.

The definition essay usually involves defining either a **concrete term** (concrete terms refer to objects or events that are available to the senses) or an **abstract term** (abstract terms refer to ideas or concepts; they have no physical referents). With a **concrete term,** your definitions would probably involve facts that you would either have to know or be able to find through research. In addition, you may need to define a concrete term any time you use a word that is not common knowledge. For example, if you are writing about a medical condition using technical words, you may need to define the terms. This would be using the concrete form of the word. For example, in a discussion of Alzheimer's disease, if you talk about "amyloid plaques," you would need to clarify for the reader that these plaques are a small abnormal patch of protein found in the brain. This kind of clarification is done within the essay to help clarify terms for your reader.

For **abstract terms,** whose meaning varies according to the person who is defining the term (this is known as a stipulative definition), you may have to draw upon different things in order to define your concept. A very simple word can have many complex meanings. For example, the word *good* is an abstract word. What does it mean to be "good"? Are there degrees of "goodness"? You can imagine writing an essay defining the abstract concept of "goodness" by researching different cultures, different time periods, and different religions in terms of how each group defines "goodness." Abstract terms, because they are more complex than concrete terms, require even more vigorous and detailed definitions. Remember, this is an argument, so your task is to prove what you believe the word *good* to mean, and you do so using research and proof.

A definition essay needs to be clear so that the reader understands what you are defining. You need to use explanations, descriptions, analysis, specific examples, and any quotes from research in order to prove your definition. Although you can make an entire essay out of this technique, this is especially useful inside larger essays. Do not forget that when writing any kind of essay, if you need to define a term or clarify an idea, you are using the definition technique. This will help make your ideas and arguments clear for the reader.

Here are some additional tips for writing definition essays and paragraphs:

1. Select a term to define and then focus on particular conditions or circumstances that you will use to extend the definition. Brainstorm all of your ideas, including the dictionary definition, common usages, or social definitions.

2. Use your opening paragraph to formally define the term and explain your particular approach to it. Though a definition does not need to come from the dictionary, you want to be complete in your explanation of the word. This can include the origins of the word and how it has changed over time. This is a perfect place to use the definition method for your introduction (see Chapter 5).

3. Etymology, the study of how a word has changed its meaning over time, can be an important part of your essay. Be sure to do the research needed to discuss everything accurately.

4. Did you define abstract ideas, concepts, and unique terms within the essay itself, even if the essay you are writing is different than a definition essay? Sometimes you need to elaborate and clarify an idea within a larger essay, forcing you to use the concepts here within a paragraph of a longer work.

CHAPTER 9 ACTIVITIES

The best way to understand the definition essay is to practice writing one. Below are several choices. Choose one that interests you, brainstorm the topic, create a working thesis, and write an essay defining your concept.

1. Define the word *hero.*

2. Define the word *leadership.*

3. Define the word *freedom.*

4. Define the word *equality.*

5. Define the word *government.*

6. Define the word *food.*

7. Define the word *friendship.*

Name: _____ Date: _____

Brainstorm

_____

_____

_____

_____

_____

_____

_____

_____

_____

_____

_____

_____

_____

_____

_____

_____

_____

_____

_____

Name: _____   Date: _____

Thesis

_____

_____

_____

_____

_____

_____

_____

_____

_____

_____

_____

_____

_____

_____

_____

_____

_____

_____

Name: _____   Date: _____

Support

_____

_____

_____

_____

_____

_____

_____

_____

_____

_____

_____

_____

_____

_____

_____

_____

_____

_____

_____

The following student sample, written by Steven Gomez, is a response to the writing prompt "Social Responsibility." Since this is a definition essay, the student developed a definition of social responsibility and set out to prove it. Notice the use of examples throughout the essay—not only does Steven explain the definition, but the example further proves the meaning of social responsibility.

Gomez 1

Steven Gomez

English 101

10/22/2008

Social Responsibility

According to *Entrepreneur Magazine,* social responsibility means, "Acting with concern and sensitivity, aware of the impact of your actions on others, particularly the disadvantaged" ("Social Responsibility"). Although this definition was offered by a magazine dedicated to the business world, social responsibility extends to other aspects of our world. Social responsibility is innate in most people and it begins at birth. Celebrities, in particular, use their money to give back. One example is the rapper Jay-Z who donated one million dollars to the American Red Cross for Hurricane Katrina survivors (Pinho). Although most people are born with it, not everyone fulfills their responsibility to society. Some people even become part of the problem, such as the leaders of the company Enron, an electricity provider, who submitted false information to the state of California costing consumers and utilities tens of billions of dollars in 2000 and 2001 (Gerth). The responsibility people bare should be fulfilled by everyone, even if our individual ideas of social responsibility differ. Society's problems would diminish if everyone contributed in a helpful and thoughtful way.

Individual ideas of social responsibility differ, but as a whole, most people find it important to contribute to the betterment of society. Today, high school students are required to complete community service as part of their requirement to graduate. The California Scholarship Federation is a recognized program that mandates students to do community service as well as maintain good grades in order to graduate with honors. This community service is needed in order to teach the students about the importance of giving back to one's community. Forcing students to fulfill this requirement helps strengthen their social responsibility and builds good moral character while improving their community through their volunteering. The community service that these students do can benefit them when applying to colleges, but also gives them a sense of their social obligation. That social obligation the individual learned will help all of society in the future.

One's obligation to society can be fulfilled in various ways through volunteering time, donating to charities, or getting involved in the community. Giving back to one's community would lead to a better quality of life for

Gomez 3

everyone. It is inhuman for people to have no clothes on their back, have no safe place to sleep, or die from starvation, especially children. That is why it is crucial for the fortunate to help those not as fortunate. Otherwise people would be eating out of the garbage, sleeping on the streets or under bridges, stealing, breaking into homes, and begging on street corners for handouts, not just in our country, but around the world. For example, Angelina Jolie and Brad Pitt are humanitarians who have donated one million dollars to help kids that have been affected by war ("Angelina Jolie & Brad Pitt $1 Million To Kids Affected By War"). Half of the money that they donated was for refugee children in Iraq. The money provides school supplies and educational programs for these kids. The other half of the money will go to American children who have lost a parent in Iraq or who have a parent currently serving in the Armed Forces. What motivates Angelina Jolie to give back is her sense of moral obligation. In the *Washington Post* Jolie said, "My visit to Iraq left me even more deeply convinced that we not only have a moral obligation to help displaced Iraqi families, but also a serious, long-term, national security interest in ending this crisis" ("Angelina Jolie & Brad Pitt $1 Million To Kids Affected By War"). Jolie and Pitt are celebrities who donate in order to fulfill their social responsibility, but even governments have an obligation to be socially responsible. From January to May of 2008 many fields dried up due to drought leaving a shortage of food in Africa, which led to millions of people dying of hunger (Kuyera/Perry). The U.S. government contributed eight hundred million dollars to Ethiopia in 2008 to help the hungry in Africa. These are two examples of individuals and governments who are changing the lives of those without basic necessities.

Becoming part of the problem or not contributing to the solution is failing to fulfill one's social obligation. In a poll done by Harris Interactive Inc. only one third, or thirty one percent of adults, believed that they had a "personal responsibility to make the world a better place by being actively involved with various issues and causes" ("Social Responsibility: Most People Have Good Intentions But Only A Small Minority Really Practice What They Preach"). The poll was conducted online in 2007 by 2,383 adults who were eighteen years or older. That is a low percentage of people who feel a responsibility to society. This number could be lower since not everyone practices what they preach. It is a scary thought that most people do not feel obligated to contribute or help society, but it is worse when someone adds to existing problems. For example, Saddam Hussein was found guilty of killing 148 people in Dujail. He was tried for genocide for killing up to 100,000 people by poison gas in 1988 ("Hussein Was Symbol Of Autocracy, Cruelty In Iraq"). This is definitely not the way to fulfill one's social responsibility. In fact,

Saddam Hussein went in the opposite direction. In no way did Saddam Hussein improve society. Instead, he ruled with an iron fist, which benefited only him and he would kill anyone who opposed him. Hussein was an individual who was not socially responsible, but this can also be true of companies and their leaders as the case of Enron proves. Instead of pushing and moving society forward to improve the quality of life, those who ignore their social responsibility and act out of greed only hurt society.

Everyone has a social responsibility to contribute, regardless of what motivates them to do so. The fact that high school students are required to do community service shows that social responsibility is significant in our society. There are different ways to fulfill that responsibility such as donating money like Angelina Jolie, Brad Pitt, and the U.S. government. Yet, there are ways to make society worse by ignoring one's social responsibility like Saddam Hussein and Enron. Because giving back is more beneficial, it is important to fulfill our social responsibility. Doing this will help everyone in all societies.

Works Cited

"Angelina Jolie & Brad Pitt Donate $1 Million To Kids Affected By War."
usmagazine.com. US Magazine, 25 June 2008. Web. 20 Oct. 2008.

Gerth, Jeff and Richard A. Oppel. "Enron Forced Up California Prices,
Documents Show." *The New York Times.* The New York Times
Company, 7 May 2002. Web. 20 Oct. 2008.

"Hussein Was Symbol Of Autocracy, Cruelty In Iraq." *cnn.com.* Cable News
Network, 30 Dec. 2006. Web. 20 Oct. 2008.

Kuyera/Perry, Alex. "Pain Amid Plenty." *Time Magazine* 18 Aug. 2008. Print.

Pinho, Domenique. "Celebrities Donating Millions." *The Loquitur.* Loquitor,
14 Oct. 2005. Web. 20 Oct. 2008.

"Social Responsibility: Most People Have Good Intentions But Only A Small
Minority Really Practice What They Preach." *Harris Interactive.* Harris
Interactive, Inc, 18 June 2007. Web. 20 Oct. 2008.

"Social Responsibility." *Entrepreneur.* Entrepreneur Media, Inc, 2008.
Web. 20 Oct. 2008.

CHAPTER 10

Compare and/or Contrast

Imagine you are ready to buy a house. You begin by looking at many different houses. After seeing a few dozen homes, you narrow it down to two choices. Once you have a detailed inspection report from both homes, you sit down to look at your options. Both houses are nice and both houses meet your requirements. So how do you decide? At this point, your mind begins to create a list of attributes for each house. Which house is in better condition? Which house has more space? Which house has a bigger backyard? Which house is a better deal? As you answer these questions, you are consciously comparing and contrasting the two houses. What better way to decide than to create a list comparing and contrasting all the different aspects of each house? Understanding this natural connection between two objects is the starting point for comparing and contrasting.

Note: Unless otherwise specified, when you see a writing prompt that says compare/ contrast or compare and/or contrast, it implies that you may compare, contrast, or both. Keep that in mind as you continue reading this chapter.

The **comparison and/or contrast essay** shows similarities and/or differences between two persons, places, things, or ideas. It makes use of the same techniques of comparing and contrasting that we use in our daily thoughts and conversations. Brainstorming becomes an act similar to choosing a house—write down all the things each object has in common and all the things each object has that are different. In most cases, you choose something over another because of your natural ability to compare and contrast.

Although comparing and contrasting two things is normal, the process becomes more difficult when you are asked to compare and contrast abstract ideas (see Chapter 9). For example, in a college class, you may be asked to compare and contrast two different presidents of the United States. The two presidents you choose to write about might have different hair color. However, that is not something you would want to write about in an academic essay. Normally, when asked to compare and contrast something, you will be writing about ideas, concepts, and philosophies that need to be analyzed. Instead of writing about hair color (a physical attribute that is obvious when you look at two presidents), you should focus on how the two presidents dealt with an issue facing the country (this would make a much better essay). This means that just because something *can* be compared and contrasted does not mean you *should* write about it.

Comparing and contrasting requires an argument, which is why it is better to analyze and interpret complex ideas rather than obvious attributes. Your thesis will usually reflect this comparison or contrast, so be conscious of how you want to approach your topic. You are trying to convince the reader that there is something worth comparing or contrasting.

The way you structure your essay depends on the topic you choose. For example, let us say the assignment is to compare and/or contrast two universities. Immediately, there are some ideas you should be able to brainstorm. When looking at two universities, you might want to examine the faculty, the student body, athletic programs, location, cost, clubs and activities, academic focus (what majors they offer), and scholarships offered. However, a list like this is simply comparing or contrasting two physical attributes of the colleges. What is missing is an argument. You need to create a reason to compare and contrast these two colleges. What kind of thesis could you write that would need a compare and contrast essay? You could write, "University A is better than University B because of its academic focus." This would be a claim of value and something that can be argued using the compare and contrast essay.

In addition, the use of transitional phrases is very important in this kind of essay. Here is a re-cap of some of the important transitions you might need from Chapter 6:

Similarity:
comparatively, likewise, similar, moreover

Contrast and Comparison:
by contrast, conversely, instead, likewise, on one hand, on the other hand, on the contrary, rather, similarly, yet, but, however, still, nevertheless, in contrast

Using the idea of comparing and/or contrasting two universities (university A and university B), there are three ways to approach this kind of essay.

The following boxes represent paragraphs of thought within the essay. They are meant to help give you a visual representation of how to organize a compare (+) and/or contrast (-) essay.

1) Discuss each subject separately: using this approach, you would mention everything about University A first, including its faculties, number of students, academic courses, athletic programs, etc. in as many paragraphs as you needed. Then, you would do the same thing with University B, writing a similar number of paragraphs about similar subjects before drawing together the points in the conclusion. The conclusion would give you an opportunity to re-emphasize the things they have in common and/or the things that are different. When you write an essay using this method, you usually want to have the same number of points and support for both Universities. In the boxes below, each paragraph represents a different (contrast) between the two schools, argued from the standpoint that "University A is better than University B because of its academic focus."

Paragraph 4
University B
Faculty

-

(When contrasting in this way, be sure to connect the ideas that are contrasted from the matching paragraph earlier in the essay)

Paragraph 1
University A
Faculty

-

Paragraph 2
University A
Course and majors offered

-

Paragraph 5
University B
Course and majors offered

-

Paragraph 3
University A
Student body and clubs on campus

-

Paragraph 6
University B
Student body and clubs on campus

-

2) Discuss each subject point by point: with this method, you could divide the body of your paper into many paragraphs, discussing both University A and B in each paragraph. For example, paragraph 1 would discuss the faculty. Paragraph 2 would discuss the courses and majors offered. Paragraph 3 would discuss the clubs on campus. You could continue with paragraph 4, discussing the success rate of graduates in the workforce. Then the conclusion would tie together the similarities and the differences found in your topic. You would essentially dedicate each paragraph to one piece of support for your topic. Within the concluding paragraph, you would talk about both universities and you could compare or contrast.

Paragraph 1
University A and B
Faculty

+

(This discusses what the two universities have in common)

Paragraph 3
University A and B
Clubs on campus

-

Paragraph 2
University A and B
Course and majors offered

-

(This discusses what the two universities have in contrast)

Paragraph 4
University A and B
Graduate Success Rate

-

3) Using a combination of the two methods: instead of putting together a paragraph that talks about one topic for both universities, you would do something similar by using two paragraphs. For example, you would talk about University A in terms of its faculty. Then, in the next paragraph, you would talk about University B in terms of its faculty. This allows you to keep your thoughts organized while maintaining your comparison and contrast in close proximity. Then you would continue using this format. You would use one paragraph to discuss University A in terms of its courses and majors. Then, you would have a second paragraph about University B's courses and majors. Typically, the two paragraph pair would compare or contrast. You would follow this pattern throughout the body of your essay.

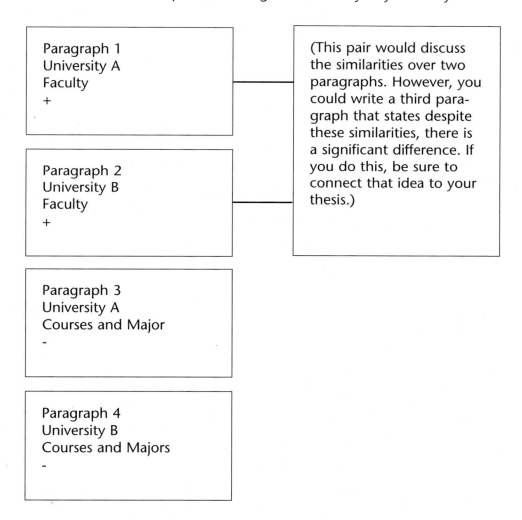

Each method explained has its place in academic writing. For example, using method 1 would be a problem for a seven-page essay. The reader may forget all the points you made in the first half of your paper. Your comparisons and contrasts would lose their effect. However, within a larger argument essay, you may find yourself relying on this method in order to present an argument between two ideas. This means that method 1 is useful in other essays besides just compare/contrast.

Some students struggle with method number 2 because it makes each para-graph very difficult to write and to keep focused. The paragraph can become very long. However, like the first method, it is very useful in a larger essay. Spending time writing one paragraph that both compares or contrasts can help prove a point as you argue your thesis.

I find that most students end up using method number 3 because it helps them remain organized throughout their essay and allows them to clearly state compar-isons and contrasts. It allows you to remain focused as you move from one example to another. Since the paragraphs follow each other in terms of the logic behind com-pare and contrast, the essay often flows in a clear manner.

Finally, it is important to note that in compare and/or contrast essays, your con-clusion is very important. In the conclusion, you are going to make sure that you clearly state the comparisons and contrasts you intended throughout your essay. So it is more than just a summary of your paragraphs. You need to clearly show the reader that you understood the things your topic had in common or the things they had that were different.

Here are some additional tips for writing a compare and/or contrast essay:

1. When you brainstorm, choose items that are related in some way so they can be compared or contrasted. If you place the subjects you want to write about next to each other in a list (see Chapter 3), you might see more things that they have in common or are different. It also might help to use different strategies while brainstorming, like tackling one subject at a time before writ-ing about the other.

2. Most things that you will be asked to compare and/or contrast in college deal with abstract ideas and serious concepts. Do not compare and/or contrast obvious things, and do not compare and/or contrast irrelevant things. In order to write a good compare and/or contrast essay, be sure to research your topic. The research you do will often reveal more topics the two ideas have in common.

3. Once you understand your topic, choose the method you want to use in order to write the best essay possible. It is up to you on how you want to approach your essay.

4. Whichever methods you choose, be sure to give equal treatment to those topics you are discussing in your essay. For example, if you give four exam-ples for University A, then you should give four examples for University B.

CHAPTER 10 ACTIVITIES

Here are some topics to think about and write a compare and/or contrast essay.

1. Compare and/or contrast two fictional characters. They can be from movies or books. In order to do this, you will need to really brainstorm a great deal in order to find ideas related to two characters. In other words, they must be characters that can be compared and contrasted.

2. Compare and/or contrast organic food to "normal" food. "Normal" is food that we buy on a regular basis that is not specifically labeled as "organic." You may want to define *organic* as part of your essay.

3. Compare and/or contrast a two-year university (community college) to a four-year university.

4. Compare and/or contrast "American Football" and "International Soccer." You may need to explain several elements that make each unique, which would require process essay methods.

5. Compare and/or contrast a few of the philosophies of a Republican and a Democrat.

6. Compare and/or contrast what music means in different cultures.

7. Compare and/or contrast different marriage rituals.

8. Compare and/or contrast rural life to urban life.

9. Compare and/or contrast different techniques for saving the environment from global warming.

10. Compare and/or contrast parenting techniques (parenting philosophies) used to raise children.

Name: _____   Date: _____

Brainstorm

_____

_____

_____

_____

_____

_____

_____

_____

_____

_____

_____

_____

_____

_____

_____

_____

_____

_____

156

Name: _____   Date: _____

Thesis

_____

_____

_____

_____

_____

_____

_____

_____

_____

_____

_____

_____

_____

_____

_____

_____

_____

_____

Name: _____ Date: _____

Support

_____

_____

_____

_____

_____

_____

_____

_____

_____

_____

_____

_____

_____

_____

_____

_____

_____

The following student sample, written by Kate Cruzat, is a response to the writing prompt "Compare and/or contrast public schools to private schools." This is a common debate, especially amongst parents. As you read, notice how Kate organizes the arguments—nearly every paragraph has a common argument. However, Kate strongly believes public schools are better. By using compare/contrast essay techniques, she is able to prove this argument.

Kate Cruzat

English 68

19 Oct. 2009

Why are Public Schools Better?

Within American society, schools are a significant influence in a person's life. The education and standards that schools present act as a guide to one's growth and development. Schools teach students the essential knowledge and basic skills that will help them become successful in the future. Schools also help build one's character through the regulations, beliefs, and actions that are demonstrated in the school's environment. However, many people do not realize that the environment of a school greatly depends on the type of school a student attends. When it comes to reality, public schools are more beneficial than private schools because of the diversity it exposes to students. The exposure to the surroundings of a public school serves as an essential fundamental in shaping a student's character.

The diversity in public schools is a better way to develop a student's open-mindedness than in private schools because of the quantity of people enrolled in the system. Since a public school provides free education in a community supported by public funds, the majority of the people choose to attend this type of school. The great amounts of people receiving education in a public school allow students to cooperate and associate themselves with many others who have "dissimilar" beliefs and values. By being exposed to these other beliefs and values, a person has the chance to understand and accept people that are different. According to an Internet article, "In fall 2009, a record of nearly 49.8 million students in America will attend public elementary and secondary schools" ("Fast Facts"). Approximately fifty million students in the United States will be educated in public schools. The vast number of students that attended school in 2009 gives these students the opportunity to meet different kinds of people with different religions, morals, and race. As a result, students learn to accept others' outlook in life despite their own views. The familiarization of various perspectives in life will influence them to be respectful human beings, which will prepare them for the future when they encounter people with other beliefs. Thus, the vast quantity of students in a public school is an excellent way to construct one's social personality.

Cruzat 3

Furthermore, unlike public schools, the small amount of students in private schools hinders the opportunity to interact with a variety of different views. The lack of students will reduce the chances of socializing with people with dissimilar morals and beliefs. Rather than being aware of certain differences between each human being, students in a private school will merely interact with people that are similar to them due to the small number of students. For instance, a private Catholic school, such as St. Lucy Priory High School, may not accept students with a different religion. Therefore, students can only collaborate with students with the same religion as them. According to an Internet article, "… 5.8 million students are expected to attend private schools this fall" ("Fast Facts"). The estimated six million students that are attending private schools in 2009 is much less than the number of students attending public schools. As a result, the importance of learning to cooperate with others regardless of their sex, religion, and morals would not be practiced as much as it would be practiced in a public school. Therefore, the number of students in a private school affects the students' social skills and understanding of other views.

In addition, the teaching credential requirements for public schools emphasize the significance of a teacher's influence on a student. In order to be a public school teacher, teachers are required to have their teaching credential completed and approved by the state. Therefore, it is clearly evident that public schools have qualified and educated teachers who are prepared to make a difference in a student's life. Grace Chen, who often writes about public and private schools, says, "Teachers in public schools are state certified... training required by the state including student teaching and coursework. They are required to hold college degrees and to be licensed by the state." The fact that a public school teacher must have a college degree, along with the appropriate training and certification by the state, reveals the high-quality education they teach to students. With the proper teaching credentials, public schools display their teachers as trustworthy, capable professionals. Hence, the qualities of the teachers in public schools create an important and positive influence towards students.

Conversely, the teacher qualifications in a private school are not as rigorous as a public school. Most private schools do not demand teachers to obtain a certification to teach. Since private schools are under the financial and administrative control of a private body or charitable trust rather than the government, states do not require teachers to have training. Usually, private school teachers merely have a broad subject expertise. The lack of a specific certification could indicate deficiencies in the teacher's abilities, which does not benefit the student's learning. For instance, a teacher with no certification or

Cruzat 5

training may not be prepared to discipline a student in an appropriate manner. In this example, it is possible to have multiple students misbehave at the same time, disrupting the classroom setting. As a result, students can become an impolite people because their teacher lacks disciplinary skills. Therefore, teachers with no certification and/or training in private schools can unknowingly affect a student's behavior in a negative way.

Moreover, public schools often give students the freedom to wear clothes of their choice, enabling individuals with the right to express themselves. Although an appropriate dress code must be respected and obeyed, students are still able to wear garments they yearn as long as it abides by the school's set of rules regarding the students' acceptable attires. Due to the liberty to dress differently, students are able to express their unique individualities to each other. Concerning the issue of school uniforms, Matthew Sirpis states, "Young people often express their feelings through the clothing that they wear… If we want individuality, freedom, and comfort for students… we should not have a school uniform policy for students who attend public schools." In today's youth, many people portray their emotions and thoughts through their appearance; school uniforms discourage students' right to enjoy and show their distinctive characters. Additionally, the ability to wear regular clothes can put the student in a more comfortable mood. As public schools

Cruzat 6

exhibit the diversity of people's styles, students enhance their creativity and originality.

On the contrary, the stricter dress code regulation in a private school limits one's identity. Rather than presenting one's artistic self through clothing, private schools make students wear uniforms. Assigning students to wear uniforms disallows the students to freely reveal their emotions to others. Public and private schools both have a dress code regulation in order to abolish any negativity that can be messaged through one's apparel. Nevertheless, the stern limitations in private schools restrain students' opportunity to discover and explore other people's uniqueness. According to Alastair Endersby, "Uniform suppresses individualism… rather than encouraging teachers to recognize their different characters and abilities…students to accept aspects of their own lives." Uniforms cause the environment of the school to be identical, which disables teachers to distinguish their students' personalities. This is important because uniforms in private schools often stops a teacher from customizing educational material and it stops a teacher from speaking directly to a student based on mutual likes/dislikes. In other words, a teacher will not even know a student's favorite color if everyone is wearing a uniform. Thus, the rigorous limitations of dressing in private schools confine a student's freedom, discovery, and identity.

Cruzat 7

The differences in private schools and public schools do affect a student's character. The diversity in public schools allow students to socialize with more people, which results in a better acceptance and awareness of a variety of opinions. The small number of students enrolled in private schools hinders one's chance to relate with different kinds of people despite their religion, gender, and race. In addition, the certification and training of teachers in public schools greatly depict their advanced teaching skills in comparison to private school teachers. The required uniforms in private schools inhibit students' imaginative thinking to liberally convey themselves through their clothes. Thus, the versatile atmosphere in public schools serves to be a more positive, encouraging influence in constructing one's quality.

Cruzat 8

Works Cited

Chen, Grace. "Public School vs. Private School." *Public School Review.* Public

School Review LLC, 04 Dec. 2007. Web. 23 Oct. 2009.

Endersby, Alastair. "School Uniform." *International Debate Education*

Association. IDEA Inc., 27 May 2009. Web. 24 Oct. 2009.

"Fast Facts." *nces.ed.gov.* National Center for Education Statistics, 01 Aug.

2009. Web. 23 Oct. 2009. <www.nces.ed.gov/fastfacts/display.

asp?id=372>.

Sirpis, Matthew. "Should Students Have To Wear School Uniforms?" *Ezine*

Articles. Ezine Articles, 07 Apr. 2005. Web. 23 Oct. 2009.

The following student sample, written by Evelyn Sandoval, is a response to the writing prompt "Compare and/or contrast several cultural aspects of two different ethnic groups." This writing prompt is very vague, so the student brainstormed in order to get a focused thesis. Notice how the student uses the compare and/or contrast essay methods in this essay. What is Evelyn really doing, comparing or contrasting? What does it do for the argument in the essay? Also, you should notice how good research and support from outside sources can strengthen any kind of essay. In addition, you should notice how Evelyn carefully chooses her words in what can be considered a controversial topic.

Sandoval 1

Evelyn Sandoval

English 101

10-29-08

Surviving in America

America is a large country consisting of many ethnicity groups who emigrate from all over the world. Latinos, for instance, form 15% of the population in the United States, which is about 45.4 million people. According to statistics, Hispanics are the second largest ethnic group in America ("Hispanic/Latino Profile"). Another ethnic group that is growing in population is the Asian group. Asians make up 5% of the population in the United States ("Asian American Profile"). Statistic rates obviously show that Latinos compose a higher percentage of population in America than Asians. These two different ethnic groups are very different in cultures, age groups, economy, and

Sandoval 2

life style. It is possible that many people from these groups shared the same experience of coming to America from another country. Both of these groups have made a big difference in America, yet they have different backgrounds from each other. Asians focus on education as one of their biggest priorities when coming to America. Asian families are not as large as Hispanic families because Asians take time to prepare economically and thus, have a smaller family with a stable life style. Today, we see Latinos spend more money on non-necessities items compared to Asians because Asians take care of their money. There are many important businesses that are created and owned by Asians, which in return, makes our economy grow. Cultures, religions, backgrounds, and life styles often influence how Hispanics and Asians want to prepare for life. In general, Asians are more reserved and take their religions and cultures more seriously because they often pass this knowledge to the next generation. As a result, Asians become more successful in America compared to Latinos. Asians tend to get a better education and work for a happier life in America.

Asians make education one of their first priorities in life. Not all cultures take education seriously. This is why many people do not make progress in America—without education, some people stay poor. Asian groups are known for their knowledge and fast learning in school. They are usually very

Sandoval 3

successful in the math and science fields. For example, in college, we see

many Latinos struggle in math classes while Asians dominate. It is reflected

by their high scores and class advancement. On the SAT tests for 2008, growth

among Asians made up the 61% of students taking the test (Nealy). In 2006,

the rate of Asian high school dropouts was 9.3. The percentage of Hispanic

high school dropouts was 22.5 ("Fast Facts"). This shows that Hispanics

dropouts are more than doubled compared to the Asian groups. This difference

shows an alarming trend amongst these two cultures. Therefore, according to

statistics, it is noticeable that Asians take education more serious than

Hispanics, which has a great affect on how future generations of these cultures

view education.

    Many Latinos come to America with other priorities besides education.

They come looking for the American Dream that will make them succeed in

life. For them, that American Dream becomes years of hard work. They focus

on trying to get a stable job to survive in this country. Latinos tend to work

overtime and earn minimum wage salaries with many "blue collared" jobs. For

example, we often see workers cleaning freeways, picking up trash, doing con-

struction jobs, or any other hard, dirty, and physical job. It is not often that we

see an Asian group working on the streets doing the same manual labor.

Hispanics represent about 33% of the labor force that work part-time jobs

Sandoval 4

(Lazo). In contrast, we see Asians with many "white collared" jobs like computer technicians, assistants, sales representatives, doctors, management positions, and other types of secure professions. These jobs often grow and enrich the individual's lifestyle. In 2003, data showed that most professional jobs were performed by Asians. For example, in the computer engineer field, 72% were Asians and 2.5% were Hispanics (Le.). These percentages show the impact that Asians have on this field. Asians tend to be more determined and successful in certain employment fields. Again, these statistics show an alarming trend and continues to demonstrate the differences between the two cultures.

Family life is also a contributing factor when comparing Asians to Hispanics. A family size can affect how decisions and futures shape their lives. In many circumstances, Asians families are not as large as Hispanic families. For example, a family composed of both parents and two children is the average for a normal sized family. A smaller family can provide more economic stability. Statically, Hispanic families are composed of numerous members beyond four people. Asian families have an average of 5 members. In 2007 there were 3,320 Asian families with no more than 5 members. Hispanics for instance, had 10,332 families composed of 5 or more members ("Bureau of Labor Statistics"). These statistics show that Hispanic families tend to grow

Sandoval 5

more in size. Another example is the pregnancy rates within today's society.
Young teenagers are the most affected by this situation. Girls between the ages
of 15–20 are sexually active and may conceive unwanted pregnancies. We
commonly see young pregnant Latinas affected by this fact more than Asian
women. The Hispanic pregnancy rate in 2007 between the ages of 10–20 per
1,000 females was 55.3, whereas, the Asian rate was 15.3 (Mrela). This is a
tremendous difference between both ethnic groups. It shows that Asian
females are more responsible and take care of themselves. For Hispanic
females who get pregnant at a young age, they often dropout from school and
do not continue with their education. In 2007, the rate for Asian dropouts in
California was 9.7. For Hispanics, the rate was 25.2 ("High School Graduates
Completing College Preparatory Courses, by Race/Ethnicity: 2007"). That
dropout rate difference between both groups further shows how the two
cultures differ. It demonstrates that Asians take education more seriously when
compared to Hispanic students. In this case, family and education can work
together to influence the future generations of these cultures.

Community as a whole is very important in society; Asian communities
are very strong and large in America. Generally, they concentrate on their
businesses and continue to grow in a stable economy. Asians like to have a
healthy life, live in a good environment, and try to take the right path in life

Sandoval 6

with little problems. For example, in some parts of America, it is rare to see Asians involved in gangs, on the streets causing damage and involved in murders. In contrast, many Hispanic ethnicities have different gangs. Most of the time we see Latinos implicated in fights, causing damage to the community, doing graffiti and committing crimes. In 2000, out of 548,517 gang members 255,254 were composed of Hispanic and 34,296 were composed of Asians (Carlie). This means, there were 220,958 more Hispanic gang members. That is an enormous difference between these two groups and it proves that Hispanics are more involved in gangs than Asians. For example, one of the biggest gangs in the United States is MS13, composed of Hispanics from El Salvador and parts of other Central America countries. The members are known for having tattoos all over their bodies. This gang is on the verge of becoming the first gang to be categorized as an organized crime entity. The MS13 are violent and spread fear everywhere they go. In 2005, the FBI arrested 660 MS13 from all over America (Barco). It is sad to see how Hispanic people can produce violence and crimes. Because of these facts, it reveals that Asians tend to stay away from problems and crimes. The greater the number of people involved in crime, the greater impact it has on that culture.

Sandoval 7

Culture also contributes to how every country sees education and its citizens succeed in life. Education is an important value in many Asian cultures. In every country, families have their own way of how to educate their families and what kind of advices should be given. Many Asian immigrants first come to America for colleges and universities. In fact, some even come for a graduate degree. Hispanic countries also value education and try to put it as one of the priorities in life. One of the differences between Hispanics and Asians is that Hispanics are more "liberal" with their free time and tend to leave for last what should be a priority. For example, in Asian countries, when school time is over, students go to after school programs, stay for tutoring at school, go to the library, or spend the rest of the time studying. In contrast, we commonly see Latinos go to soccer practice or spend time with their friends outside school. Asian students take education as a priority and put it before anything else. This is why Asians succeed more than Hispanics in school and in their life.

In conclusion, by comparing and contrasting how Asians and Hispanics live their life in America, we see that, in general, Asians have a better educated life and become more successful than Hispanics. Asian groups put education first. They are taught that education has to be their first priority. When they come to America, their goals are to continue with their education and live

Sandoval 8

in prosperity. We see Hispanics with other goals besides getting an education. They are concerned more about supporting their families and working as many hours as possible to save money. Asian groups are more likely to have a smaller family and give them as much attention as needed. Statistics show that Hispanic families are often composed of more than 5 members. This affects Hispanics by not giving the proper attention and economic stability to their children. Hispanics put other priorities before education. Rates of Hispanic school dropouts are a lot higher than Asians, which determines their future. As a result, Asians become more victorious in their ability to survive and prosper in America. Asians enjoy a better life style, exist in a better economic class, and give their families a better life.

Sandoval 9

Works Cited

"Asian American Profile." *The Office of Minority Health.* U.S. Department of
Health and Human Services, 27 Jan. 2009. Web. 4 Apr. 2009.

Barco, Mandalit. "The International Reach of the Mara Salvatrucha." *npr.*
National Public Radio, 17 Mar. 2005. Web. 28 Oct. 2008.

"Bureau of Labor Statistics." *Bureau of Labor Statistics.* United States Bureau
of Labor Statistics, 2008. Web. 28 Oct. 2008.

Carlie, Mike. "The Racial and Ethnic Composition of Gangs." *Into the Abyss:
A Personal Journey into the World of Street Gangs.* Michael K. Carlie,
2002. Web. 28 Oct. 2008.

"Fast Facts" *IES.* National Center for Education Statistics, 2008. Web. 28 Oct.
2008. <http://nces.ed.gov/FastFacts/display.asp?id=16>.

"High School Graduates Completing College Preparatory Courses, by
Race/Ethnicity: 2007." *kidsdata.org.* Lucile Packard Foundation, 2008.
Web. 28 Oct. 2008.

"Hispanic/Latino Profile." *The Office of Minority Health.* U.S. Department of
Health and Human Services, 12 Mar. 2009. Web. 4 Apr. 2009.

Lazo, Alejandro. "Hispanics Hit Hard As Workers Lose Hours." *The
Washington Post.* The Washington Post Company, 1 Sept. 2008. Web.
28 Oct. 2008.

Sandoval 10

Le, C.N. "Employment and Occupational Patterns." *asian-nation.* Asian
Nation, 2008. Web. 28 Oct. 2008.

Mrela, Christopher K. and Jose Jimenez. "Teen Pregnancies." *azdhs.gov.*
Arizona Department of Health Services, 1999. Web. 28 Oct. 2008.

Nealy, Michelle J. "College Board Reports Most Diverse Class of SAT Test-
takers on Record." *Diverse.* DiverseEducation.com, 27 Aug. 2008.
Web. 28 Oct. 2008.

CHAPTER 11

The Problem Solution Essay

Have you ever opened the morning newspaper and discovered the world is full of problems? Then, do you think to yourself, "Why haven't they tried my solutions?" The connection between a problem and the solution in our society is tied to an individual's beliefs and feelings about the topic. However, when presented in an essay, the goal of the writer is to convey clearly what the problem is and what solutions can be offered. When writing this kind of essay, you have to be both knowledgeable in the subject and logical with your solutions. For example, if you were writing about a problem within society, and your solutions are controversial, then it is your responsibility to present those solutions in a logical and coherent manner. In essence, you are trying to persuade somebody that your solutions will work. Likewise, if you were making a claim that a problem exists that people are ignoring, then you need to be just as persuasive in making your arguments.

When starting a **problem solution essay,** I recommend that you think of it as two separate essays before you begin writing. It helps to brainstorm two separate ideas. First, brainstorm the problem that you want to address. Then, brainstorm the solutions to that problem. When you see the connections between the ideas you want to write about, you may need to brainstorm again in order to get your ideas focused.

Usually, a problem solution essay follows the format where the problem comes early in the essay, followed by the solutions. If, for example, you only need one paragraph to explain the problem, then the rest of your essay would focus on your solutions. Sometimes, the problem needs to be clearly explained, which may require several paragraphs in your essay. Then you would offer the solutions towards the end.

The following boxes represent elements of thought within the essay. Unlike the compare/contrast essay, these are *not* paragraphs. These boxes are designed to show you the proportions of arguments in your essay. In other words, they represent the amount of discussion for problems and solutions.

Problems (the majority of your paragraphs deal with the problems of your topic)	Problems
	Solutions (the majority of your paragraphs deal with the solutions you are going to make for your topic)
Solutions	

OR

On occasion, you may need to write an essay that does not offer any solutions. You would be writing one essay dealing with only the problems about your topic. This happens in newspapers when people write letters to the editor. Or, when you need to persuade a large group of people that there is a problem, you will try to convince people they need to take action. Your essay might look like this:

Problems (this is not one paragraph, but rather many paragraphs convincing your reader that there are problems that exist for your topic)

As you move through these chapters, you should begin to notice a few patterns. First, all essays contain arguments. And second, and most importantly, you use the different essay styles together to write effective essays. For example, when explaining your problem or your solution, you may need to rely on the process-analysis essay in order to clearly explain what you are talking about within a paragraph. Provide examples whenever necessary, and be sure to research any additional information that will help support your positions. You want your solution to be as "realistic" as possible and as logical and tenable as possible.

Here are a few things to keep in mind before, during, and after you write a problem solution essay.

1. If the problem is a complicated one, is it broken down so the reader understands all it involves? Your job is to clearly communicate the problem, so be sure to completely analyze and discuss the problem. Your brainstorm will often reveal what approach you will take, and knowing which pattern you will follow will help organize your essay.

2. If solutions are being emphasized, are the ones presented viable enough for the reader to believe in? In other words, solutions should not be based on "tractor beams" and "science fiction." Your solutions need to be as real as possible, proven through research and expert opinions.

3. Research is important in all essay writing, but within this kind of essay, it is extremely important to find out what others have to say about your topic. Did you research the topic enough to understand most of the problems and the solutions? If you have a narrow understanding of the problem, you may be offering simple solutions. This is especially important in order to avoid solutions that people have tried and are known to fail.

4. Although the diagrams in this chapter show unequal proportions for a problem/solution essay, it is possible to write an essay with equal problem and solution paragraphs. For example, you could have 3 paragraphs on problems and 3 paragraphs of solutions.

5. In addition, it is also possible to alternate between problems and solutions. The structure does not have to start with only problem paragraphs, then solution paragraphs. There are many essay topics that might need a different pattern that includes a problem paragraph followed by a solution paragraph throughout the entire essay. This is especially useful in other types of essays.

CHAPTER 11 ACTIVITIES

Now, we should practice writing a problem solution essay. Below are a few top- ics to choose from. Choose one that interests you, do a full brainstorm, and write an essay that addresses the problems and solutions you deem necessary based on that topic.

1. Address a problem at a place where you have worked and offer solutions to that problem.

2. Address the problems and solutions older people face when they are unable to care for themselves.

3. Discuss the problems and some of the solutions in selecting a career before going to college.

4. Discuss some of the problems and solutions Wal-Mart faces when they try to open a new store in a small town.

5. Choose a problem related to your campus (like parking, class size, fees) and write a problem solution essay.

6. Politics and government are always a great place to find problems. Explore some contemporary problems and offer solutions.

7. Discuss some of the modern problems with healthcare in America and offer some solution. You may reference other healthcare systems used by other countries.

8. Discuss some of the current problems our education system faces and offer some solutions. You may want to focus on a specific level of education, like high school, in order to offer specific solutions.

9. Discuss some of the problems and solutions related to labeling animals as endangered species.

10. Discuss some of the problems and solutions related to addiction. This is a broad topic, so you will want to focus on a particular kind of addiction. You will also find this topic in other chapters, which means you can use other essay methods in combination with your problem/solution essay.

Name: _____   Date: _____

Brainstorm

_____

_____

_____

_____

_____

_____

_____

_____

_____

_____

_____

_____

_____

_____

_____

_____

_____

_____

186

Name: _____   Date: _____

Thesis

_____

_____

_____

_____

_____

_____

_____

_____

_____

_____

_____

_____

_____

_____

_____

_____

_____

_____

_____

_____

188

Name: _____   Date: _____

Support

_____

_____

_____

_____

_____

_____

_____

_____

_____

_____

_____

_____

_____

_____

_____

190

The following student sample, written by Mayra Iniguez, is a response to the writing prompt "Address the problems and solutions associated with divorce." In this essay, notice how Mayra begins the arguments with the negatives of divorce, but concludes that there are positives of divorce (and how that actually proves her thesis). As you read, notice how the essay is organized in terms of problems and solutions. Finally, notice how Mayra uses support throughout the essay, relying more on summary than on direct quotes.

Iniguez 1

Mayra Iniguez

English 061

12 Dec. 2009

The Parental Influence in Children from Divorced Families

About 40% of children experience parental divorce (Amato). In the wake of the new divorce phenomenon, many researchers have increasingly strived to gain a wider understanding of its prevalence and effects. Divorce, in general, has been stigmatized and considered deviant. Some scholars perceive that a two-parent family is the norm because it produces healthy, competent, normal and productive citizens (Amato). Moreover, as society shifts away from the traditional family, there has been a wider acceptance of divorce. With divorce, there emerges the debate about the effects it has on children. Many people believe that divorce is a stressful experience that has negative repercussions on children. Nonetheless, the positive parental influence on children can be the marker in alleviating the traumatic effects of the divorce, and thus contributing to a child's overall constructive adjustment. This is important to understand because it is counter intuitive to what most people believe about divorce.

The majority of studies assert that the result of divorce has countless negative consequences. Divorce has been perceived to supersede multiple social problems, especially for children. The intense experience of divorce on children has been said to be extremely overwhelming and traumatic. Contenders have argued that divorce has a negative impact on children; it affects them emotionally, behaviorally and mentally (Amato). This experience can cause the child long term harm that can be carried into adulthood. At times, the divorce can be so overwhelming on children that it manifests into violent, aggressive or depressive behaviors, and in extremes cases lead to suicide (Eleoff). A large pool of studies from the 1990's contends that children from divorced parents will "score lower than children from continuously married parents on measures of academic success" (Amato). The reason students from divorced parents are said to achieve less is due to the impact and disrupt that divorce causes. In conjunction, the disintegration of parents may result in poverty and or forced to live in less desirable areas in order for the parents to make ends meet. This downgrade of living arrangement sometimes constrain the family to migrate to "ghetto" or deteriorating neighborhoods that predispose the children to gangs or other deviant behaviors. Most research argues that substance abuse, emotional, and psychological problems for children or teens are a direct result of dysfunctional homes where divorce is typically present.

Divorce can be severely detrimental on children. To a child, divorce can be like a "death" in the family. This stressful event can manifest itself into negative consequences. A disruption such as divorce can have long term consequences on a child's overall well being. The functionality of a well adjusted child that experiences divorce might in turn result in destructive and harmful behavior. Divorce might affect a child's self image, create depression and elevate psychological problems that were never seemingly present prior to the divorce ("The Effects of Divorce on Children"). Larry Bilotta, author of several books on marriage, discovered that after a parental marriage breakup, most "children tended to be lonely, unhappy, anxious and insecure." Many children are inadequately prepared for the severely changing event of a divorce, and their grief and vulnerability predisposes them to greater risk of substance abuse, smoking and other social problems. Bilotta argues, "Seventy percent of long term prison inmates grew up in broken homes" where divorce was seemingly present. This reaffirms that divorce can truly have a serious impact on a child that may be extended into adulthood.

Iniguez 4

Not all children or individuals are the same nor react the same when it comes to divorce. The severity and extent of the consequences of divorce vary by individual and external factors. The traumatic event of divorce might result in a decrease in children's grades or psychological well being, but might not last forever. Any traumatic or devastating event will result in negative consequences during that phase, but things typically return to normal after some time (Eleoff). The length and duration of the effects might last longer for some people depending on the individual, not necessarily because of divorce itself. Several protective factors can shield children from being severely affected by the divorce. The mother plays a vital role on how the child copes and deals with the divorce (Amato). In regards to the negative impact of academic achievement, this might not always correlate to the divorce itself, but rather to the child's overall intellectual abilities (Bilotta). During a divorce, a child is vulnerable and susceptible to its effects, but the magnitude depends if the bond of the parent-to-child relationship has been disrupted (Hughes). Furthermore, other reactions seem to be influenced by the age of the child. The younger the child, the more likely he/she are to be able to easily transition from the divorce. Younger kids typically do not know how it is like to live and have a nuclear family so they will not be as affected. Children from "three to five years of age believe they have caused their parents' divorce" (Eleoff). These

Iniguez 5

children feel "self blame" and are more likely to experience emotional effects such as depression and insecurities about the future ("Emotional Effects of Divorce on Children"). Despite the age, all children need to feel support, and gain reassurance from both parents that they did not cause the separation in order to ease the transition.

The effects of divorce can be less devastating for the child if the transition is made smoothly. While it is clear that divorce can be truly detrimental in multiple aspects of a child's life, parents can be the marker of how the child copes with the divorce. Parents can lessen the effects by helping their child "deal with the stresses and painful feelings divorce creates" (Raab). Following a divorce, the most important thing parents can do is to ensure that their children feel loved, appreciated, and ensure the children that the divorce was not their fault. This might not completely eradicate the nostalgic symptoms, but could definitely play a role in how children cope. During the divorce, many children experience a wide range of emotions, because to a child, the unimaginable has happened, and the child is in a state of confusion. Therefore, much research has indicated that although parents divorce each other, it is imperative to remember that they did not divorce the child. This suggests that both parents need to continually be supportive of the child and actively involved in the child's life ("The Effects of Divorce on Children"). In conjunction, although divorce can create a battle for both parents seeking custody of the child, it is imperative that even though the parents might not get along, that they both remain close and participate in all the day to day activities of the child ("The Effects of Divorce on Children"). Having both parents involved in the day to day life of the children could ease tension and help the children cope with divorce.

It is usually in the child's best interest to have two happily married parents, but at times, divorce is inevitable and might actually be beneficial for the child in the long term. Divorce can be a traumatic and stressful experience, but "represents a second chance for happiness for children to escape from a dysfunctional home environment" (Amato). Based on this, it is important to understand that at times, divorce (rather than parents forcing each other to stay together in an unhappy marriage) is more beneficial for the children. In instances where there are high levels of conflict and or violence within the home, the divorce is better for the children and everybody else's well being. Research has indicated that, "the most damaging effect of divorce on children is the emotional trauma caused by parents who fight or battle each other" ("Emotional Effects of Divorce on Children"). Sometimes all this chaos at home distorts the child's perception of a family. In the long term the child will suffer more by remaining in an unhappy home where he/she might potentially take on the conflict resolution techniques and extend them into their relationships as adults ("The Effects of Divorce on Children"). A dysfunctional home does not have to consist of divorced parents. A dysfunctional home can also be derived by an unhappy marriage that creates an aversive home environment. When parents minimize the conflict, limit the hostility, and focus on providing a positive child rearing, they can contribute to the child's growth despite a divorce.

The adjustment of a child going through parental divorce can be complex. The child is very likely to experience an array of mixed feelings such as anger, loneliness, and depression or other emotional and psychological problems. The joint living arrangements have been suggested as the norms and the safe heaven to create productive and healthy children, but at times there are drawbacks to this arrangement. Many times having the parents separate might be more beneficial for the child in the long run because the family dynamics might intrude with their healthy growth. Furthermore, the effects of the children's adjustment after the divorce have more to do with the quality of parental relationship sustained with the child after the divorce. Divorce is a depressing stage that can be extremely tough on the children, and it is the parents' responsibility to help ease any and all negative feelings that the children of divorce are dealing with.

Iniguez 8

Works Cited

Amato, Paul & Alan Booth. "The Consequences of Divorce for Attitudes

    Toward Divorce and Gender Roles." *Journal of Family Issues* 1991.

    Print.

Bilotta, Larry. "The Hidden Effects of Divorce on Children." *Ezine@rticles.*

    EzineArticles.com, 2010. Web. 21 Mar. 2010.

Eleoff, Sara. "An Exploration of the Ramifications of Divorce on Children and

    Adolescents." *The Child Advocate* Nov 2003: A1. Print.

"Emotional Effects of Divorce on Children." *Deal with Divorce* 2009: A1.

    Print.

Hughes, Robert. "Divorce and Children." *ParentNews* 1999: A1. Print.

"The Effects of Divorce on Children." *Family & Consumer Resources* 2009:

    A1. Print.

The following student sample, written by Julia Dominguez, is a response to the writing prompt "Depression." This writing prompt is very vague, so the student brainstormed in order to get a focused thesis and then chose how to organize the essay. You should also notice how this essay includes methods from other essays. Can you spot some of the different styles in this essay?

Dominguez, Julia

English 68 TTH

Depression

Life brings us all kinds of moments—some days might be bad, and others might even be worse. When these kinds of days start to pile up, we get overwhelmed, and some of us latch on to certain emotions when we are not even aware of it. More and more people are becoming so affected by the chaos and hardships of life that it is leading to depression. Depression is a disease that covers a variety of symptoms, all having to do with mood changes, loss of pleasure, and an overall negative outlook on life. It is often confused with overwhelming sadness or a large amount of stress. Sadness and stress is a huge factor of depression, but it does not define it or replace it. This misconception is a substantial problem, because if people are not aware that they are depressed, then they will not seek the help that they so desperately need. Depression has become so widespread in our society, that it is often called "the common cold of mental illnesses." Aside from being common, it is also one of

Dominguez 2

the most treatable of mental illnesses, which gives this condition hope. Because depression is such a growing dilemma, researchers have studied it intricately, and found that there is actually more than one kind of depression. This means that there are also a number of solutions.

One of the most dominant types of depression is called "major depression." In order to be diagnosed with this type, one must show five symptoms that are present for at least two weeks. Some of these symptoms include sadness, stress, a sense of worthlessness, hopelessness, or a change in behavior, such as a change in eating habits and sleeping patterns. All of these symptoms may seem familiar in our lives. That is why depression is so common, because most of us feel like this at one point or another. As a matter of fact, major depression affects "15 million American adults, or approximately 5 to 8 percent of the adult population in a given year" ("About Mental Illness"). The complications with this depression can be utterly severe. According to an internet source, "completed suicide occurs in up to 15% of individuals with severe Major Depressive Disorder. There is a fourfold increase in deaths in individuals with this disorder who are over age 55" (Long). The overall cause of depression is unknown to researchers, since it is different with each individual. However, common triggers may be death of a loved one, a loss of a job, or an end to a relationship. The lasting effects of major depression vary depending on the severity, but the "lifetime prevalence for this disorder in the general population is 10% to 25% for women and from 5% to 12% for men" (Long). A lifetime can feel like forever, especially for someone suffering from depression. If depression is dealt with appropriately, a lifetime of it may turn into a one time experience.

The second form of depression is called "dysthymia," which is defined as a "mood disorder" (Juhn). This type of depression is more chronic and also long term. In fact, "Unlike major depression, dysthymia may last for years" (Sue 352). It has basically the same symptoms as major depression, which consists of sadness and a lack of hope or worth. The key difference is that with dysthymia, the main focus is the amount and quality of sleep that the person has. In other words, 25% to 50% of people who suffer from dysthymia usually have evident sleep abnormalities (Juhn). For instance, impaired sleep continuity and reduced rapid eye movement causes a loss of quality sleep cycles. Dysthymia has been researched time and again, and one of the more crucial studies shows that "each year, about 10 percent of individuals with dysthymia go on to have a first major depressive episode" (Sue 352). Dysthymia can be extremely long lasting, and when it comes to sleep deprivation, it can be torturing. The effects can last anywhere from 2 years to a lifetime, though "overall, the lifetime prevalence is about 6 percent" (Sue 352). If there is reason to

Dominguez 4

think that dysthymia may be to blame for a severe change in sleep habits, it is to your advantage that you seek help before it can get worse.

The person themselves is not the only one who suffers from their depression. Most of the time, the burden of the disorder is passed on to family and friends. It is hard enough to see someone you love feel unhappy, what is worse is when it gets so bad that they cannot function properly throughout the day. When it gets to this point, family members and friends do whatever is possible to help get that person through it, and back to a healthy way of living. This only becomes a problem, when the person who is depressed either refuses to accept their help, or refuses to make an effort to change at all. It is then that those people who care so much, and worry constantly, have nothing else to contribute, and no where else to turn, but the other way. If someone is not willing to accept help or support, then those family members and friends that were once there to turn to, will eventually give up on them, and accept the fact that, "this person is not going to change and there is nothing I can do about it." Many times, depression can start with a loss of a loved one, and cause the loss of a loved one as well.

It is hard to concentrate on other things when something distressing is on one's mind. This does not change in the work environment, or any environment for that matter. This holds true, with someone who is going through depression, and still has the obligation of going to work. If the depression is severe enough, over time, it will start affecting the person's work habits, and may eventually lead to the loss of their job. They may start to be late more often because they just do not care to be on time. They could do a poor job on a certain task because it does not seem important to them anymore. A job is demanding, whether it is manual labor, or a business like atmosphere. Coworkers and employers have other priorities to attend to, and dealing with one's depression is unfortunately not one of them. If one's depression is affecting the business in a negative way, most likely, that person will be out of a job. It does not matter how compassionate the employer may be; their main concern is maintaining the welfare of the business, and if that means losing an employee, then so be it.

Not being able to confide in those that you love, and suddenly becoming unemployed may lead to a number of emotions, not to mention a more serious form of depression. It may all of a sudden seem like there is nothing left to live for. When the negative effects of depression start to appear, the person will eventually lose even more. They will lose their self esteem, ambition, confidence, and ultimately their sense of self. Not only will they have no family member or friend to turn to, they will sooner or later not even have themselves. All of these effects can be prevented, if the depression is detected early

Dominguez 6

enough for it not to have caused any permanent damage, and if the person going through the depression is willing to get help. As long as this is recognized, there is still hope for a healthy and happy future.

There are various solutions to help triumph over depression. Two of the most commonly practiced treatments are cognitive psychotherapy and antidepressants. Both are effective, and can also be quite similar. For example, "brain scans show that antidepressant drugs increase metabolism in certain brain areas, and successful psychotherapy produces almost the same changes" (Kalat 469). Someone who is suffering from depression should look to any kind of solution that works for them. Kalat writes, "When depressed patients get no treatment at all, about one third improve over time anyway. If given antidepressant drugs, about two thirds improve. If given cognitive therapy, again about two thirds improve. If given antidepressant drugs and cognitive therapy—guess what—still two thirds improve" (469). Evidently, seeking help—no matter what kind of help that is—turns out to be the most beneficial choice.

The primary solution is to undergo cognitive psychotherapy, which is a series of therapy visits to help become reacquainted with the positive aspects of life, rather than the negative. The advantage of this is that there is no need to take medication, and "in comparison to drug therapy, psychotherapy has one

Dominguez 7

important advantage: Someone who recovers by means of psychotherapy is less likely to relapse into a renewed episode of depression" (Kalat 469). The convenience of antidepressants is hard to argue against, but the long term benefits of cognitive therapy seem to be of more value. There are many approaches to therapy when it comes to depression. Two of the most effective kinds available are cognitive-behavioral and behavioral. Cognitive-behavioral therapy helps people through a procession of three major steps. First, they help identify a patient's negative views about themselves, the world and the people around them. Second is to develop alternative ways of viewing certain life experiences, and third is to "rehearse new cognitive and behavioral responses" that they can carry with them through everyday life (Erbaugh). Behavioral therapy includes a lot of scheduled training techniques to help bring the focus to a more assertive way of life. The patient may be asked to self evaluate their experiences and moods throughout the day or to attend certain social events to improve communication and to encourage a more active lifestyle. Many times within a session, they may perform a number of relaxation exercises to create a less stressful environment. One's mental health is something that cannot be taken lightly. Its affects spread throughout a person's life in a damaging and sometimes fatal manner. So, despite the fact that cognitive psychotherapy may not be the more convenient or financially favorable method, it is simply the

Dominguez 8

safer and more permanent method. In addition to being the longer lasting form of a solution, there is also outside involvement to monitor a person's well being. According to the article, "Benefits of Psychotherapy for Depression," when there are scheduled therapy visits:

> Psychotherapy can be exceedingly helpful in monitoring and managing suicide risk and compliance with both medical and psychosocial intervention programs. Moreover, it can be beneficial in dealing with impairments of psychosocial function and reactions to stress, disappointment, loss, bereavement, and the other psychosocial issues that are common triggers or consequences of the persistence or recurrence of depression. (Erbaugh)

With a person consistently there, who is able to analyze a patient's progress, they are able to intervene if a situation gets out of control. The expert helping will know what to do and how to proceed. This way, when life unexpectedly changes, someone using therapy techniques will have a support group to help offer solutions.

Antidepressants are a form of medication that helps reduce the amount of depression, and are usually used when the depression is so severe that there is no other way to overcome it. The many antidepressant drugs that are available fall into four major categories. Of those categories, Tricyclics and Selective Serotonin Reuptake (SSRI) are the ones that have been known to be the most successful. Tricyclics work with the neurotransmitters within the brain. They stimulate certain cells and receptors, and block others (Kalat 466). For instance, one receptor that they block is histamine, which usually produces drowsiness. Selective serotonin reuptake inhibitors are types of antidepressants that are most commonly used. They are similar to Tricyclics, but work specifically with the neurotransmitter serotonin (Kalat 466). Typical SSRI's that may be prescribed are Prozac, Luvox, Zoloft and Celexa (Kalat 467). Cognitive Psychotherapy is the primary source of help, only because it does not affect your body directly, and the side effects do not relate to your physical health. According to Kalat, "Drugs, however, have their own advantages. They are cheaper than psychotherapy and more convenient" (469). The convenience lies within the fact that the benefits start to show between "2 or 3 weeks, whereas the benefits of psychotherapy generally develop gradually over 2 months or more" (Kalat 469). In today's society, most of us are always on the run and busy dealing with day to day responsibilities. For those of us who relate to busy lives, it seems more convenient to take a pill rather than spend an hour a week talking to someone about your depression.

Dominguez 10

Depression is a disease; it is something that most of us cannot help but dwell on when it has shown its face. It can be overlooked and not taken seriously, and if this happens, there may be damaging consequences. Many of us are aware of the signs of depression, and the penalty of it, but there are those of us who are in denial. We think, "Oh, I'm mentally stable, I'm just going through a hard time right now, I'll get over it," when in reality, it may just get worse. So when the madness of life takes its toll on us, and we find ourselves weighed down by our own emotions, we need to look at the signs and come to terms with the fact that it may be depression, and if so, then we need to seek help. The information is out there—we just have to take the initial steps, and go from there. Depression *can* be cured; there are many ways that we can get help. If we refuse to believe, or deny that this may be true, it could eventually lead to ineffectual lives, and heartbreaking realities.

Dominguez 11

Works Cited

"About Mental Illness." *nami.* National Alliance on Mental Illness, 2009. Web.

3 Apr. 2009.

Erbaugh, Susan E. "Benefits of Psychotherapy for Depression." *Healthy Place.*

Healthplace.com Inc., 2009. Web. 3 Apr. 2009.

Juhn, Greg, David R. Eltz, and Kelli A. Stacy, eds. "Major Depression Health

Article." *Healthline.* Healthline Networks, inc., 2009. Web. 3 Apr.

2009.

Kalat, W. James. *Biological Psychology.* Canada: Wadsworth, 2004. Print.

Long, Phillip W. "Major Depressive Disorder." *Internet Mental Health.*

Internet Mental Health, 2005. Web. 3 Apr. 2009.

Sue, David, Derald Wing Sue, and Stanley Sue. *Understanding Abnormal*

Behaviors. Boston: Houghton Mifflin Company, 2003. Print.

CHAPTER 12

The Cause and Effect Essay

Class is dismissed and you walk to your car. You get in, put the key in and turn the ignition. Nothing happens. You try again. The car just sits there. The thought processing part of your brain kicks in—if I turn my key and my car will not start, I must have a dead battery.

The moment you make that connection is the moment you understand how cause and effect work. Understanding cause and effect begins with the why. Why do certain things happen? What is the result of things that happen? When you begin to ask these kinds of questions, you are beginning to think about the *relationship* between cause and effect. After you turned the key, you recognized that nothing happened. This is the effect. You think that you have a dead battery because, normally, this is one of the primary causes of a car not starting. It is what you have been told about cars. The dead battery is probably the cause of the car not starting. But is it the only cause? What other things could go wrong and make your car not start?

Doing this exercise is great practice for starting an essay. The same ideas apply—look at the ideas and concepts involved with a cause and effect relationship. This is what you want to brainstorm. This is what you will prove through argument in your essay.

The example of your car shows a simple cause and effect relationship. It demonstrates a chain of events in the physical world. When writing an essay, oftentimes you are asked to analyze much more complex cause and effect relationships—like why people use harmful drugs. Discussing a cause and effect relationship about drugs is far more difficult than explaining why your car will not start.

The cause and effect essay focuses on a situation or condition, and then asks either "why," which are the causes, or "what are the results," which are the effects. Since your aim in writing a cause and effect essay is to offer a good explanation of some relationship, it is necessary to think about the topic thoroughly. For example, if your paper is on the causes of insomnia, you might relate it to things like too much caffeine, medicines that keep you awake, a long hard work day, stress from a relationship, a sick relative, or many other factors. You could always research some of these causes and the potential effects of not sleeping at night.

A cause and effect essay should always deal with possible causes or effects, as long as you make it clear that your ideas are only plausible rather than definitive. In other words, you can discuss potential causes and potential effects, as long as they are in the realm of possibility. This happens often in many areas of our lives because, in essence, you are being asked to evaluate and determine relationships between ideas that not everyone may agree on. The cause and effect essay is even more of an argument essay than the others we have encountered.

The cause and effect essay is similar to the problem and solution essay. They follow the same organizational patterns. You could have an essay dealing with many causes for one effect. Likewise, you could have an essay dealing with many effects based on one cause. No matter what, a cause and effect essay needs to have both elements in the essay. Since cause and effect have a direct relationship with each other, you should be sure to include both in any essay that uses these techniques.

The following boxes represent elements of thought within the essay. Unlike the compare/contrast essay, these are *not* paragraphs. These boxes are designed to show you the proportions of argument in your essay. In other words, they represent the amount of discussion for cause and effect.

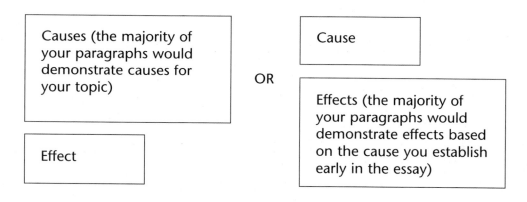

Although these diagrams show the general focus of your essay, there is another technique that is very useful inside a larger essay. In other words, it is possible to explain cause and effect by breaking down each paragraph into a cause followed by a paragraph about the effect. You could also combine the cause and effect into one paragraph. For example, you could write your essay like the one on the following page:

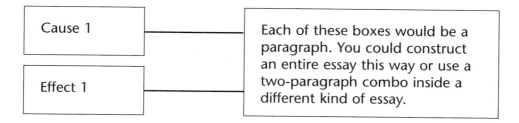

Or,

Cause and effect can be done in one paragraph, which is extremely useful in essays that combine the different types. You could also construct an essay using paragraphs like this.

Here are a few tips and strategies to remember when writing a cause and effect essay:

1. When you brainstorm, compile a "chain" of causes and effects to help deter-mine their relationship and to see how the causes and the effects all are related to each other. This "chain" becomes the core argument in your essay. It is the connection of these ideas that you want to try to prove in your the-sis. Your thesis should reflect exactly what causes and effects are important to your topic. Since you will probably be talking about important social issues, your thesis will naturally include why your discussion of the causes and effects is important.

2. Make sure that your evidence is reliable and accurate. Remember, just because one event happened before another does not mean one was the cause of the other. This is a common mistake, so always trace your logic to make sure it is accurate. This will help you avoid a common fallacy called "False Cause." This fallacy happens when an argument assumes a causal rela-tionship without sufficient evidence. For example, suppose you write the fol-lowing argument: "Every severe recession follows a Republican Presidency; therefore, Republicans are the cause of recessions." This would create the "False Cause" fallacy because it can be easily argued that there are many other factors that cause a recession, not just the one in your argument.

3. Remember to use important transitional words to make your paper flow as you discuss the chain of causes and effects. See Chapter 6 for some key transitional phrases appropriate for this kind of essay writing.

4. Summarize the chain of cause and effect in the conclusion by making direct reference to your introduction and by restating the chains you established in terms of the cause and the effects. Since there is a connection, use your conclusion to reinforce the causal relationship to your reader and to clearly show how the ideas are connected.

5. Although the diagrams in this chapter show unequal proportions for a cause/effect essay, it is possible to write an essay with equal cause and effect paragraphs. For example, you could have 3 paragraphs on causes followed by 3 paragraphs on effects.

CHAPTER 12 ACTIVITIES

Now, you should practice writing a cause and effect essay. Below are a few topics to choose from. Choose one that interests you, do a full brainstorm, and write an essay that addresses the causes and effects you deem necessary based on that topic.

1. Discuss the cause and effect of gambling. You can focus on the community, a family, or the individual.

2. Discuss the cause and effect of two people getting married at a very early age. Look at some of the social issues involved.

3. Discuss the cause and effect of teenage suicides. This may require some research since people argue about the causes on a regular basis.

4. Discuss the cause and effect of dishonesty, such as cheating or stealing, in the classroom or in the workplace.

5. Discuss the cause and effect a recession has on society. You can focus on businesses or individuals.

6. Discuss the cause and effect of worshiping "heroes" in pop culture. These "heroes" can include music, TV, and movie stars. You can also think of athletes as pop culture heroes.

7. Discuss the causes and effects of bullying. This can be the traditional school bully, or you can apply this topic to a new kind of bully, the "Internet" bully.

8. Discuss some of the causes and effects of the rapid increase in obesity in America (or the world). Avoid the easy argument: people are obese because they eat too much. You may want to take a psychological approach in order to write a strong argument.

9. Discuss the cause and effect of modern technologies. This is a broad topic, so you might want to focus on a specific technology, like the medical field. Remember, the cause and effect for this topic can be positive and negative.

10. Discuss some of the causes and effects that advertising has on children. These can be ads from television, print, or radio. In addition, you should focus on the type of product (like a toy or food) being marketed to children.

Name: _____   Date: _____

Brainstorm

_____
_____
_____
_____
_____
_____
_____
_____
_____
_____
_____
_____
_____
_____
_____
_____
_____
_____

Name: _____   Date: _____

Thesis

_____

_____

_____

_____

_____

_____

_____

_____

_____

_____

_____

_____

_____

_____

_____

_____

_____

_____

Name: _____   Date: _____

Support

_____

_____

_____

_____

_____

_____

_____

_____

_____

_____

_____

_____

_____

_____

_____

_____

_____

_____

The following student sample, written by Henry Torres, is a response to the writing prompt from this chapter's activity, "Discuss the cause and effect a recession has on society." Henry decided to do something different. Here, he argues the positive effects of a recession (even though most people argue that recessions are negative). Notice how Henry appeals to an emotional response in many of his arguments even though he is using statistical evidence in some paragraphs. You should also notice how he stays consistent to the argument in his thesis.

Henry Torres

English 101

29 Oct. 2009

The Positive Side of a Recession

Today, the word "recession" may be a frequently used word in many conversations. It is obvious many are being affected by a stagnant, poor economy. Many businesses have been forced to lay off employees who have been with the company for years. Many people have been left without a job and have fallen into debt. These people also struggle to support family, themselves, and to survive. Due to the loss of a job, many are forced to vacate the homes that they have worked so hard to obtain. It is easy to spot many of the negative affects of a recession by watching the news or even talking to strangers. However, it is important to discuss the fact that not everyone is affected negatively by a recession. People should be aware that something good can come from a recession. Understanding the positive effects of a recession is important because many people can actually benefit from this economic pain that affects millions of people.

According to *Webster's Dictionary,* a "recession" is a period of reduced economic activity during which the level of unemployment rises, production slows, and general prosperity lags. A recession can also be associated with an economy, whereas many consumers exercise caution with their spending habits. A recession usually occurs when the balance between money supply, interest rates, and inflation is tipped. A slump or decline in the housing market or the collapse of banks in the U.S. and Europe can cause consumer confidence to become weak. As production inventory increases and the demand for goods decreases, many businesses have to cut costs and unneeded expenditures, such as jobs, resulting in a recession.

Although many are affected in a negative way during a recession, there are those who can take advantage from the downturn of the economy. Some consumers are benefiting from the cost of certain items that may have been difficult to purchase prior to a recession. For example, in the middle of a recession, the housing market begins to collapse, causing the value of homes to decline sharply. Some consumers who have been putting off the investment of a house because of a high housing market are able to purchase homes at a

Torres 3

far better price during a recession. According to data from *HousingTracker.net,* the median house price in Orange County, California, as of October 2009, was $459,000. This is compared to $694,833 in April of 2006 ("Existing Home Listing Statistics for Orange County, California"). Because there are more homes on the market than buyers, the price of homes in many areas has fallen. This is often referred to as a "buyers market," because more homes for sale mean people have more options before buying. And if the prices drop due to a recession, more and more people can afford to buy a home. In addition to homes, there are many other positive aspects of a recession when it comes to being a consumer.

Some people are also taking advantage of lower car prices, both new and used. With many people out of work trying to find ways to save money and car dealers experiencing a major drop in sales, some buyers have a wider selection to choose from and are able to negotiate a far better price during a recession, resulting in a value. For example, many car dealers are offering 0% financing for the length of the loan. In addition, many car dealers are offering large cash incentives in order to entice buyers. Furthermore, others are taking advantage of retail bargains and restaurant promotions. Many can benefit from retailers clearance sales and restaurants value menu items. For instance, many restaurants offer special deals designed to feed two people. Again, the restaurant is suffering during the recession and the drive to appeal to new and returning customers is high. This desire directly passes savings on to the customer. Finally, some people during a recession can even benefit from a vacation. A number of people are benefiting from Southwest Airline's special offer of $59 or lower one-way ticket price to and from selected cities *(Southwest.com).* Many who have been looking for the right time to purchase a home, travel or buy something that was too expensive are able to grasp during a recession.

During a recession, many people can have their work hours reduced, are forced to furlough, and even lose their jobs completely. Some people are finding the benefit of using the extra time to improve one's skills. A number of people are returning to school to learn a new trade, career, and pursue an Associate or Bachelors degree. Many are returning to colleges and universities to upgrade their job skills in hopes to secure employment in the near future. According to Catherine Jackson, Director of Research and Planning at Shasta College, "At Shasta College, enrollment in vocational courses—those typically associated with job training—has grown 7.5 percent from spring 2008." Due to the costs of tuition and fees linked with education, some are considering attending a community college over a university. In 2007, the cost to attend a Community College without a scholarship was $4552.00 compared to an

Torres 5

in-state University with a cost of $15,488.00 (Clark). A little extra time on one's hand during a recession can help many to improve their proficiency in a career and earn a degree.

Recessions can cause stress and can lead to depression within a family; however, recessions can actually be beneficial to families. This benefit is not reflected financially; instead, the benefit comes from the emotional connection from family bonding, since more time may be available to all of the family members. Family meals can have a positive effect from a recession. For example, long work schedules, working on weekends, or traveling can cause a strain on a family. For some, the extra time away from work allows one to reconnect with family members at breakfast or at dinnertime. According to *KOLD News 13,* "Americans are working fewer hours...spending more time with family" ("Can a recession be good for your health?"). Helping in the kitchen with meal preparation, cleaning up, or just being with everyone at the table can rekindle the family spirit. Recessions can also help families develop efficient spending habits that can outlast a recession. This is a great time to learn how to manage spending and live within one's means. Reading sales advertisings, cutting coupons, shopping at local thrift stores, looking for bargains, and rethinking a purchase can help families get through a difficult period. Recessions can have a positive effect on the family by encouraging unity and exercising spending techniques.

Furthermore, a recession can have a positive effect on the way some people value certain possessions and friendships. During a booming economy, many people are enthusiastic to move to new area, buy a new car, to replace one that is two to three years old, or purchase the latest fashion designer clothing and shoes. When faced with a recession, there are those who benefit by taking care of what they have. Many people maintain their older vehicles, homes, and take care of clothing and/or other items that would normally be replaced or not used. By taking care of certain items, one can prevent unnecessary purchases that usually lead to wasteful spending. Moreover, friendships can be encouraging during tough economic times because some friends may provide clothing, food, and jobs. Other friends can help to complete a home project, repair a car, get one's children to and from school, or simply offer advice when feeling depressed. Many people are finding the benefits from learning to appreciate what one has instead of what one cannot have and from having supportive friends during a decline in the economy.

Not everyone is affected negatively by a recession. Understanding the positive effects of a recession can help one to take advantage of learning new skills, uniting a family, manage spending, or purchasing a home. Usually, a

Torres 7

decline in the economy is stressful for many people. During a recession many

struggle to find work, while others are simply trying to survive. But a

recession should not always be considered negative. In spite of this dark

economic cloud, many people are finding ways to prosper during a recession.

Torres 8

Works Cited

"Can a recession be good for your health?" *kold.com.* World Now and KOLD, 2009. Web. 27 Oct. 2009.

Clark, Kim. "College Tuition Prices Continue to Rise." *U.S. News and World Report.* U.S. News and World Report, 23 Oct. 2007. Web. 23 Oct. 2009.

"Existing Home Listing Statistics for Orange County, California" *Housingtracker.net.* Creative Commons Attribution Share Alike. Web. 20 Oct. 2009.

Jackson, Catherine, "During a Recession People Return to School for New Careers." Ed. Rob Rogers. *The Record Searchlight Redding.com.* Scripps Interactive Newspaper Group, 24 May. 2009. Web. 18 Oct. 2009.

"Recession." *Webster's Online Dictionary.* Phillip M. Parker, INSEAD, 2009. Web. 17 Oct. 2009.

Southwest.com. Southwest Airlines Co. 2009. Web. 18 Oct. 2009.

The following student sample, written by Kai Wu, is a response to the writing prompt from this chapter's activity, "Discuss the cause and effect of dishonesty, such as cheating or stealing, in the classroom or in the workplace." In this case, Kai decided to focus on academics. As you read, notice how Kai takes a very serious tone for something that many students do not really take seriously. In addition, notice how he uses the techniques in this chapter in order to prove the severity of the argument. By the time you get done reading, you will probably never cheat again!

Kai Wu

English 68

14 Nov. 2009

Academic Dishonesty

Education is one of the most important issues concerning the nation. Education not only determines a person's worth, but also represents the nation's power. Powerful nations such as United States put great effort into designing the educational system. As people become more aware of the importance of schooling, it is up to the individual to pay attention and be an active learner in the classroom. Unfortunately, academic dishonesty (such as cheating) has been on the rise in past decade and has become one of the most common offenses committed by students. The intense competition in society and expectations from others burden the students with heavy pressures to achieve academic success. As a result, students resort to cheating in order to meet these expectations. Such behavior greatly undermines the education system and can ruin the bright future of any student who cheats. Therefore, it is necessary for students and those in the academic field to understand the causes and the effects of cheating in order to confront the problem.

A leading cause of academic dishonesty is the expectation from the parents. The majority of society agrees with the idea that education is essential for career success and that academic success often leads to a prosperous future. Since most children do not have the ability to make prudent decisions, parents have the responsibility to direct their kids onto the right path. In an article that discusses academic dishonesty, Drew Bush states, "The main cause of students committing academic cheating is the fear that they have of disappointing their family, especially their parents." The idea that academic performance has been emphasized at home has been deeply rooted in the American culture and has influenced people's ways of raising their children. Parents expect their kids to succeed in school and often punish their kids for failing to do so. As a result, children suffer from enormous pressure and often turn to cheating in order to meet the expectations.

Another source which causes students to cheat is stress from intense competition at all academic levels. As a family's financial resources become more abundant, many people now have the opportunity to send their children to school or even attend school themselves. The end result is that the more educated people there are, the more competition that exists among those people. This includes the competition for classes and for jobs later in life. Anyone who cannot keep up with the academic demand and expectations might be considered a failure. According to Drew Bush, "The fear of not keeping up with peers… is another reason why high school students and some college students commit such a serious offense." Educational achievement represents a person's status because it is often associated with a successful career. In other words, people who fail academically have greater chance to fail in their future and are looked down upon by others. The stress coming from the competitive environment escalates until the point where students give up trying and resort to cheating as the solution.

One of the most immediate and devastating effect of cheating is that it can ruin one's academic career. In order to be accepted into top colleges, students often cheat on exams, such as the SATs and ACTs. However, those who cheat suffer serious consequences. Colleges put great emphasis on integrity and will reject anyone who cheats on a standardized test. According to one of the leading college admissions counselors, Kate Cohen, "The student could potentially be haunted by their wayward past, thus shaping their future in a not insignificant, although probably manageable, way. Those caught cheating might be forced to change their college list or consider community colleges for the first time." Top colleges turn down all dishonorable students, disregarding their exceptional performances prior to the act of cheating, since those students did not earn the scores fairly. Furthermore, any misbehavior that concerns a student's integrity will be on record where colleges can see when considering admission. Any evidence of cheating can dramatically change one's life and end academic pursuits.

Not only can cheating destroy one's academic career, it can also ruin a person's future. Cheating enables students to achieve good grades without putting forth the required effort. Although copying other's work is much easier than doing it by oneself, a student cannot learn the knowledge essential for the future with cheating. An article about the consequences of academic misbehavior points out, "Cheating is an addictive habit that will surely destroy a career even if it does not (publicly) destroy an education" ("The One Minute Case Against Cheating"). Sometimes, it is human nature to choose the easy way out. Once a student gains the perception that one can achieve goals easily by stealing other's work, the student will develop the habit of cheating. Again, cheating often takes less time and is easier to do, leading to higher scores and higher grades at the expense of learning the material. If this trend continues, this deceitful person could allow "cheating" to permeate other aspects of

Wu 5

his/her life, thus making other people despise them. Untruthful individuals could eventually lose their friends, jobs, and families.

While the educational system in United States has improved with the efforts of the government and society, cheating has remained a serious problem. Many Americans now regard education as their top priority and often ask their children to excel academically. As a result, students feel pressured and many cheat to meet their parents' expectations. Competition also burdens students with heavy stress so they have to turn to cheating for a solution. One will face enormous obstacles in academic pursuits once a student's integrity becomes questionable. Furthermore, cheating can grow into a habit and destroy one's future. Therefore, it is imperative for the public to acknowledge the consequences of cheating and establish strict rules to prevent any forms of academic dishonesty.

Works Cited

Bush, Drew. "Back to School: Facts About Academic Cheating" *Associated Content.* Associated Content, 30 Jul. 2009. Web. 14 Nov. 2009.

Cohen, Kat. "The Truth About Cheating Your Way Through Standardized Tests Success" *The Huffington Post.* HuffingtonPost.com, 09 Oct. 2008. Web. 14 Nov. 2009.

"The One Minute Case Against Cheating" *One Minute Cases.* The One Minute Case, 20 May 2008. Web. 14 Nov. 2009.

CHAPTER 13

Literary Analysis

What is your favorite book? Now, explain why it is your favorite book. What characteristics make this book special to you? Characters? Plot? Style? Are these some of the things you are thinking about? As you begin to formulate a reason why you enjoyed this book, you are beginning to make an argument. Like all the other essays, a literary analysis essay makes an argument about concepts and ideas in literature (this also includes movies, music, etc).

In this chapter, we are going to discuss **literary analysis.** Notice, this does not say we are going to learn how to write a literary analysis essay. A literary analysis essay is based upon any of the other types of essays. For example, a comparison and contrast essay or a cause and effect essay could all be types of literary analysis. Unfortunately, there is no formula I can give you on how to analyze something in literature. If you have seen the movie *Dead Poets Society,* you will understand what I mean. In the movie, the literature book instructs the class to make charts and equations to determine a poem's worth. Of course, this is nonsense. When thinking about literature, your goal is not to judge its worth, but rather its meaning. And meaning does not fit into a simple equation.

However, there are some steps we can take to make sure that you have all of the tools needed to offer the best analysis. When looking at a piece of literature, you should be thinking about two things. First, what does the work you are analyzing mean in its literal sense? This is the first step in understanding the deeper meaning of the work. After you have analyzed the material literally, it is time to think of it in more abstract and metaphorical terms. What meanings does the passage offer? What other interpretations can you offer based on its context? What assumptions based on the author, historical context, and cultural context can you deduce in order to offer an interpretation of what you are reading?

Here is an example: "The cat sat on the mat."

From a literal standpoint, what does this sentence mean? Quite literally, the sentence is telling the reader that a cat went and sat on a mat. We can picture this in our mind. We understand its literal meaning. We can agree that there is only one interpretation of the literal meaning; the cat clearly sat on the mat.

Now comes the fun part. What deeper interpretations, thinking in abstract terms and metaphorically, does this sentence mean? Why did the cat sit on the mat? Was there sun shining on this mat? Was the cat forced out of its other sitting spot? Was there no other place to sit? Was the cat told to sit there or face punishment? And what is up with that mat? Where is it? What color is it? What is the mat's deeper meaning? What or who does the cat represent? These are all questions that require interpretation.

At this point, I have no answers to these questions. The sentence has no context. However, it is possible to apply some logical inferences to this sentence. Since I know cats sleep a great deal, I can imagine that the cat chose to sit on this mat in order to go to sleep. The mat is probably in the owner's house, and probably in a main room, such as a living room or kitchen, because that is where most people keep their mats. And because cats love to lay in the sunshine, it is possible the cat is going to sleep on this mat because it is in the direct sunlight. Is this interpretation correct?

That is what makes discussing literature so exciting. The only wrong interpretation is one that cannot be supported and argued based on contextual information and on logical inferences. So although you may disagree with my interpretation of the sentence, I can certainly argue it from a logical point of view. Your point of view may be different, but as long as you can support it with examples and proof, then you have an argument for your interpretation.

We may never know what the author truly intended. That is not our job. Our job is to understand the meaning of something based on the context in which it was written. What an author means and what the author writes may be two different things. Maybe the author meant that the cat was on a "magical flying" mat and that it was soaring up to the skies. That would explain why the cat was sitting instead of prancing. Because prancing on a flying mat could be dangerous.

Here are some things to think about as you read literature, including novels, poems, and essays.

1. Look at the historical context of the thing that you are analyzing. When was it written? What was going on in history during this time? The more you understand its historical context, the better understanding you will have of some of the issues in the work. For example, a poem written in the 1700s in England reads differently than a poem written in America during World War II.

2. Look for social issues in the things that you are analyzing. If you know something about the historical context, this often helps you understand social issues that were going on at the time. If a poem was written during the Civil War, what does it say about slavery? What social issue is it addressing?

3. Try to understand something about the author's life. Oftentimes the author is writing about something personal. If you can find out something about the author's life, it will help you understand what it is the author is trying to convey. In other words, it will help your abstract interpretations if you understand where the author is coming from. In return, the insight into the author's life will give the work context into why, when, where, or how it was written.

4. When reading, look to answer the following questions: who, what, when, where, why, and how? If you can answer these questions, then you will be on the correct path to offering a coherent interpretation. Some of these questions are easier than others. For example, answering "who" is usually a straightforward affair. But answering "how" is much harder. The "how" could include the explanation of how something happened, like a plot line in a novel, or it could be answering how something was written. For example, a poem requires a different "how" than a novel.

5. Look for metaphors, analogies, and symbols. *Metaphors* make comparisons by saying something is whatever one is describing. For example, "The road was a sheet of glass." *Analogies* make comparisons by explaining unfamiliar terms with something more familiar. For example, we might compare the human brain to a computer. *Symbols* are often used by the writer to indicate deeper meaning. The more you understand the context of these symbols, the more you can work and refine your interpretation. For example, if a poet is using ice water as a symbol in a poem about love, then the water would symbolize a state of emotional upheaval, as if the poet is losing a love and feels lost. Be aware of these symbols as you read the poems at the end of the chapter.

6. When writing about literature, you need to support your claims with quotes from the source. If you make an interpretation, actually quote the thing that you are interpreting in order to support your claims. If you are offering a very complex or an obscure interpretation, that is when doing research and finding outside sources is very valuable. Chances are, somebody else has felt the same way you do and has written about it.

7. Be sure to think about other terms, like plot, theme, characters, style, and setting. If you analyze these things from the literal perspective, you will be opening up ideas that can lead to your interpretation. It helps to understand the literal meaning of the work before you understand the interpretations. And when writing about literature, you will often refer to plot, theme, characters, style, and setting in your essay.

CHAPTER 13 ACTIVITIES

Look at these poems to see what we can conclude about them. First, analyze the poems literally, then look for the deeper abstract meanings. What symbols are being used? What is the historical and social context of the poem? What do you know about the author? Once you have analyzed the poems, you will find some important themes and issues. Finally, you can write an essay offering an argument about your interpretation of these poems.

"Sympathy" by Paul Laurence Dunbar
Published in *Lyrics of the Hearthside* by Dodd, Mead, and Company in 1899

I KNOW what the caged bird feels, alas!
   When the sun is bright on the upland slopes;
When the wind stirs soft through the springing grass,
And the river flows like a stream of glass;
   When the first bird sings and the first bud opes,
And the faint perfume from its chalice steals—
I know what the caged bird feels!

I know why the caged bird beats his wing
   Till its blood is red on the cruel bars;
For he must fly back to his perch and cling
When he fain would be on the bough a-swing;
   And a pain still throbs in the old, old scars
And they pulse again with a keener sting—
I know why he beats his wing!

I know why the caged bird sings, ah me,
   When his wing is bruised and his bosom sore, —
When he beats his bars and he would be free;
It is not a carol of joy or glee,
   But a prayer that he sends from his heart's deep core,
But a plea, that upward to Heaven he flings—
I know why the caged bird sings!

"The Road Not Taken"
Robert Frost. *Mountain Interval*, 1920

Two roads diverged in a yellow wood,
And sorry I could not travel both
And be one traveler, long I stood
And looked down one as far as I could
To where it bent in the undergrowth.

Then took the other, as just as fair,
And having perhaps the better claim,
Because it was grassy and wanted wear;
Though as for that the passing there
Had worn them really about the same.

And both that morning equally lay
In leaves no step had trodden black.
Oh, I kept the first for another day!
Yet knowing how way leads on to way,
I doubted if I should ever come back.

I shall be telling this with a sigh
Somewhere ages and ages hence:
Two roads diverged in a wood, and I—
I took the one less traveled by,
And that has made all the difference.

Name: _____   Date: _____

Brainstorm

_____

_____

_____

_____

_____

_____

_____

_____

_____

_____

_____

_____

_____

_____

_____

_____

_____

_____

244

Name: _____   Date: _____

Thesis

_____

_____

_____

_____

_____

_____

_____

_____

_____

_____

_____

_____

_____

_____

_____

_____

_____

_____

_____

Name: _____   Date: _____

Support

_____

_____

_____

_____

_____

_____

_____

_____

_____

_____

_____

_____

_____

_____

_____

_____

_____

_____

_____

The following student sample, written by Julia Dominguez, is a response to reading the book *Passing* by Nella Larsen. Julia was allowed to develop her own topic. After reading the book, she found the relationship between the main character and her husband worth exploring and developed an argument based on her thoughts. Even without reading the book, you should be able to see how the student develops and defends the argument.

Julia Dominguez

English 68

05/11/07

Staying in Love or Deciding to Settle

Marriage between two people happens for different reasons. Many times it can be because of love. However, there are various situations when it is caused for more superficial reasons than that, such as security or social status. Most people would like to think the core meaning of a marriage is love, but often times it is not. There are marriages that start off as something other than love, and there are marriages that begin with the blossom of it, yet progress into something else. In Nella Larsen's *Passing*, the marriage between Brian and Irene can be seen as something less than loving. They have two children together, and have shared a life of success and value, yet one aspect that is difficult to detect, is love. What is obvious in their relationship is the amount of compromise and sacrifice, two elements that typically hold a strong

Dominguez 2

marriage together. On the other hand, for Brian, those sacrifices and compromises may be more resentful than anything else. By the end of the story, these two characters have dissolved into something else entirely, a fraction of the original marriage. Understanding how Brian and Irene interact will expose the true meaning of their marriage.

When a couple is in love, there is usually noticeable affection that is shared between them. A kiss before they part for the day, an exchange of admiring looks, or even a gentle touch of the hand. Yet throughout the entire book, there is rarely evidence of this affection that Brian conveys to Irene. They discuss each other's day, and show politeness to one another, and yet when they sit down to have a meal together there is not the faintest display of love. For instance, when the two of them are having breakfast at the table, Irene perceives every detail of Brian. She notices "the slight irregularity of his nose," and the "marked heaviness of his chin" (Larsen 54). However, as soon as he finishes all that he has to say, he simply goes back to what he is doing, and completely ignores Irene. She attempts to continue interaction as she offers him more coffee, but instead of replying with a caring, "no thank you dear," or "I'm fine dear, thank you for asking," he simply says, "'Thanks, no,'" (Larsen 56) and continues to read his newspaper. The disregard to Irene's reaction or her feelings in general is apparent throughout

Dominguez 3

the whole story. At times, it is as if they are respected friends rather than loving husband and wife.

   As a husband, Brian, for the most part, is supportive, respectful and considerate. However, there is often a sense of inferiority that Brian places upon Irene. He has respect for her, in the fact that he listens to what she has to say, and allows her to give her opinion, but as soon as she does, his word continuously outweighs hers. He considers her intelligence, but then rejects it. Irene is aware of this, and has even learned to surrender in certain discussions in order to let Brian sustain his feeling of superiority. When she and Brian were discussing the mystery about "passing," Brian was convinced that its reason for being was the, "instinct of the race to survive and expand," and that "the so-called whites" were a perfect example (Larsen 56). She strongly disagreed with this, ". . . but many arguments in the past had taught her the futility of attempting to combat Brian on ground where he was more nearly at home than she. Ignoring his unqualified assertion, she slid away from the subject entirely" (Larsen 56). She knew that he was in no place to make such generalizations, but his patronizing behavior as her husband forced Irene to relinquish her opinion completely. If Brian was in love with her, he would not only allow her opinion to be spoken, but he would also encourage her independent thinking to be as valid as his. As soon as he starts to consider that

Dominguez 4

she may be making a valid point, he ends the conversation without delay. An example of this is when he ". . . silenced her, saying sharply: 'Let's not talk about it please.' And immediately, in his usual, slightly mocking tone he asked: 'Are you ready to go now? I haven't a great deal of time to wait'" (Larsen 57). Brian not only dismisses the rest of the conversation for his own benefit, but he also mocks her as if a discussion with her is a waste of his time. If he loved her, then he would cherish their discussions together rather then discard them.

When one enters in a marriage, there are certain things to be sacrificed, either willingly or reluctantly. When dreams are given up reluctantly it often leads to a feeling of resentment, which ultimately may cause loss of love. For Brian, raising his family in Brazil was a lifelong dream. It was not until Irene forced him to believe that staying in America would be the best for him and his family. Only then did he start to feel remorse for giving up this dream. His resentment would show itself periodically throughout the marriage, to the point that Irene knew his state of mind every time. However, the internal bitterness that reflected his resentment was always present, and whether it was obvious to him or Irene, it affected the marriage dramatically. For example, his "dislike and disgust for his profession and his country," (Larsen 58) was apparent when he said, "'Lord! How I hate sick people, and their stupid, meddling families, and smelly, dirty rooms, and climbing filthy steps in dark hallways'" (Larsen 56). Whether he made it clear to Irene or not, he constantly blamed her for his unhappiness and dissatisfaction with life. How could he love someone who he held responsible for such life altering mistakes?

Raising the children was always a problem for Brian and Irene. There was a permanent disagreement regarding their protection as well as their knowledge. Irene felt that she wanted to protect her children from degrading aspects of the world such as the word "nigger." However, Brian was convinced that it was necessary for the children to be aware of such vileness in order to prepare them for the kind of life they would be forced to have. Every time the conversation of these two disagreements would come up, Brian showed an enormous amount of "scorn and distaste" (Larsen 59). Not only did he disagree with Irene, he was in a sense, angry at her for even thinking of depriving their children of such knowledge. For instance, when they were discussing whether or not they should move their kids to a different school, Brian accused Irene of making his children, "molly-coddles," and continued to yell, "'Well, just let me tell you, I won't have it. And you needn't think I'm going to let you change him to some nice kindergarten kind of a school because he's getting a little necessary education . . .'" (Larsen 60). Usually, when a married couple argues about how to raise their children, they reach a

Dominguez 6

mutual compromise. Although in this case, it causes more distance between Brian and Irene than anything else. It is through Brian's outbursts that we see his love for Irene dwindle even more.

Through the duration of the book, Irene becomes suspicious of an intimate relationship between Brian and Clare (a friend of Irene's from high school). For the most part, Irene's jealousy could be mistaken for irrational thinking, or jealous feelings turning into mistrust. On the other hand, it could be more concrete than that. There are certain insinuations that lead the reader to believe that an affair between Clare and Brian may be more plausible than not. From the start, Brian shows more support towards Clare than his own wife, especially when he and Irene are discussing Clare's intelligence. When Irene suggested that Clare might not be an incredibly intelligent woman, Brian was startled and replied with, "'Do you mean that you think Clare is stupid?'" (Larsen 88). Instead of defending his wife's feelings, he was more offended by the insult towards Clare. It seemed that throughout the entire story, Irene was put second on Brian's list of importance. While the three of them were walking up the steps to go to a party, Brian appeared more concerned for Clare rather than his wife, Irene. As Clare made a comment on how the garden looked, Brian made sure to warn her about walking in her heels. He said, "'Keep to the walk with those foolish thin shoes. You too Irene'" (Larsen

Dominguez 7

109). It was not that he was worried about Clare and her shoes, it was the fact that he put his wife second. It was almost as if the sudden additional warning was because he realized he had forgotten about her completely. If it was Irene who Brian loved, it would be her that he showed concern for by giving Irene the warning. Instead, the warning was for Clare. The suspicion that Irene held inside her was growing into such jealousy, and Brian knew that. Their relationship had become so distant that it was obvious Clare was part of the reason. And Brian's actions did nothing to dissuade Irene of her feelings.

The Harlem Renaissance was a time known for underground nightclubs and revolutions. African Americans were learning to overcome the social norms from their time, despite discrimination, and they were also discovering a way to openly express themselves as equals in society. Expression was forming throughout their music and literature, and was not only popular, but appreciated as well. It seems as if that time was full of freedom and exhilaration. However, there were other problems. Men were going out to nightclubs, playing music and dancing with women; it was inevitable that wives were going to be affected by it. It was becoming dangerously common to hear about jealous wives murdering their husbands. The domestic violence that was going on eventually became known as "women with knives" (Knadler). Brian and Irene were already having relationship problems that

Dominguez 8

were affecting his love for her, but they were also having mistrust issues that were leading Irene to become jealous and suspicious. The fear relating to the infamous domestic violence was bound to overcome Brian when he realized what was going on in his own marriage. It was just a matter of time before there was no love remaining in their relationship, much less a violent ending to it at all. This distance and lack of love in their relationship tore at Brian until all that was left was the fear of a fatal ending.

There is no question that Brian and Irene's marriage was respected and admired by many. They had two beautiful children, were successful in their careers, and were valued by their community. For an outsider, their life together may have seemed perfect. However, from an inside perspective it is apparent that their marriage may have been anything except for a loving relationship. Brian's dominance caused him to feel superior to Irene, his crushed dreams lead him to feel resentful of her, and their constant disagreements forced them to be unaffectionate and vindictive towards each other. All of these obstructions tore at Brian's love for Irene. It shred his love for her so powerfully, that his anger and resentment started to build up. He openly admitted to her what he had felt all along. When they spoke of their children, he confessed, "'I wanted to get them out of this hellish place years ago. You wouldn't let me. I gave up the idea, because you objected. Don't

Dominguez 9

expect me to give up everything'" (Larsen 104). This confession gives the impression that he has given everything up for her already and that he is tired of it. When he tells her not to expect him to give up everything, it implies the relationship between him and Clare. It is then that you realize that his marriage has finally reached its limit. Brian may have loved Irene at one point, but the truth remains strong; during their marriage, the love was lost long ago, starting with shattered dreams and ending with broken promises and closely kept secrets.

Dominguez 10

Works Cited

Knadler, Stephen. "Domestic Violence in the Harlem Renaissance: Remaking the Record in Nella Larsen's *Passing* and Toni Morrison's *Jazz*." *The Free Library*. Farlex, 2004. Web. 5 May 2007.

Larsen, Nella. *Passing*. New York: Penguin Books, 2003. Print.

CHAPTER 14

Persuasive Argument

Most people think that an argument is a verbal disagreement between two people. Even the dictionary supports this idea by stating ". . . a discussion in which there is a disagreement, dispute or debate." How many times have you heard verbal arguments grow loud, where the two participants raise their voices and shout at each other? Where their emotions take over and they verbally attack each other? This often happens in everyday life, and chances are, you may have even argued in this way today.

However, in this chapter and in essay writing, this is not the kind of argument we are going to discuss. You are not going to verbally bash someone. In terms of writing, to give an argument means to offer a set of reasons and evidence that support a claim (which you learned about in Chapter 4). Arguments are attempts to support certain views and beliefs with reasons.

Understanding arguments is important as a writer and as a researcher. When you write an essay, you need to understand what you are going to argue and how you are going to prove your thesis. As a researcher, you will encounter many different kinds of sources with different kinds of arguments. Understanding how other people write and argue is important in determining strong arguments that you want to use as support in your essay.

Your thesis is the central argument or the position you take in your essay. Once we have arrived at a thesis, your job is to provide reasons and support in order to defend that claim. Your argument essays should be written as if you are trying to *convince or persuade* someone of your point of view. You convince others by using the very same evidence that convinced you (which is why good support is important)!

For example, look at the debate about capitol punishment. If you claim "capitol punishment is wrong and harmful to society," then you have stated a claim of value (this could be a starting point for a thesis, but it would not be a good thesis in this form). This is what you believe, and this is what you must prove using the argument essay. But notice you will need to "dig deeper" into your topic. You must ask some very important questions, such as, "why is it wrong?" and "how does it harm society?" There are many other issues involved as well, such as human rights, deterrence, and whether or not criminals should be treated the same as law-abiding citizens. These are things you may want to address in your essay.

Every essay you have read in this book is an argument essay. This means that in any given assignment, you can combine the different types of essays. For example, you may need to use a paragraph or two of the definition method within a larger essay that uses compare and contrast. You should use whatever methods necessary to prove your point.

Counter Arguments

The information that follows can be applied to any kind of essay, but we will discuss it here because of how useful the information can be when trying to be persuasive. That is, when using an argument to persuade your reader, there are things you should do to be as persuasive as possible. We call these techniques *counter arguments*.

A counter argument is the argument that goes against what you are claiming. When you begin an essay, you take a stance. Your thesis reflects what you believe and what you are going to prove. You can think of a counter argument as the exact *opposite* of your thesis. Here is a tip to help you think about counter arguments: if you claim one thing, what do others do to argue against that claim? Most arguments have two (or more) sides, and although you are trying to persuade your reader that you are correct in your claim, you must be aware that there are other arguments that people believe can be used against you.

If it seems strange that you need to know the counter arguments, you are correct. When presenting the counter arguments, you do not simply include them and then end your essay. You must "*refute*" the counter argument. When you refute the counter argument, you are attempting to show that claim in the counter argument is not properly supported or that the evidence is false. You want to find something wrong with the argument so that you can show that the argument is weak. By refuting the counter argument, you will help prove and convince your reader that your argument is true. Think about it—if you explain a common counter argument, then prove it to be false, you have just made your argument that much stronger.

Presenting a counter argument then refuting it is very powerful. In fact, as a writer, you are actually controlling the reader's mind. As they read your essay, most readers will understand your point of view and see your argument. It does not mean that you are physically changing their belief. That is because your reader will be aware of what I call the *"common argument."* That is, most ideas, issues, and controversial topics are constantly debated in the public, which means people hear about the arguments on a regular basis. The arguments most commonly used for these topics are the common arguments. For any given topic, your reader will be thinking about common counter arguments. If you can prove the counter arguments wrong, you will have essentially told the reader that what they believe is wrong, leaving your argument the only persuasive argument in the reader's mind.

Doing all of this in an essay is an extremely effective way of writing. It allows you to be persuasive while still maintaining the rules of formality in essay writing. The more you know about the common arguments (both for and against), the better you can address these issues in your essay. In fact, since the counter arguments are typically common, it is a good idea to give them credit as being a good idea when you introduce them in your essay. This is why research is so important—you want to be sure to have support for the counter arguments as well. You want to treat a paragraph containing a counter argument like the rest of your paragraphs. You need to give it support through the research that you do. In addition, when you refute the counter argument, you want to use support there as well. Look back at Chapter 1— investigating all of the arguments involving your topic is very important. In doing so, you will come across many common counter arguments that you can use as support in your essay.

Using transitional phrases like "many argue" or "some people believe" is a good way to begin the counter argument. You are clearly informing the reader that you are shifting from one kind of paragraph to another. Once you establish the counter argument and you are ready to refute it, other transitional phrases, such as "although this argument has some merit" or "this argument has a point, however . . ." are very useful. It allows you to transition from one point into another so that your reader understands what you are doing.

When you write an argument essay using counter arguments and refutation, it will give your essay a distinct pattern. This is normal in an argument essay. In fact, you can use it in any type of essay. Here is a visual representation of how an argument essay might look. In this case, the following boxes represent paragraphs within the essay. They are meant to help give you a visual representation of how to organize an argument essay.

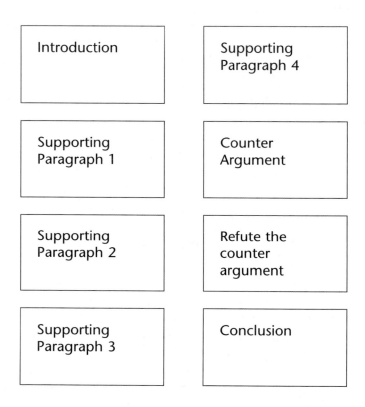

Here are a few tips and strategies for writing a persuasive argument essay.

1. In some instances, it is better to research your topic before you begin writing anything. You might learn something you did not know. New information might change your opinion. And of course, any information that is persuasive to you will also be persuasive to your reader.

2. Brainstorming is also very important in this kind of essay and it may be necessary to brainstorm multiple topics throughout the writing experience. Some students find it useful to brainstorm just the counter argument separately from the refutation.

3. There may be more than one counter argument for your topic. You are encouraged to put more than one in any assignment. If you have more than one counter argument, you should put each counter in its own paragraph. Then, you can refute both at once, or use one refute paragraph after each counter paragraph.
4. Transitional phrases are important in these kinds of paragraphs. The reader must know what each paragraph is trying to communicate. Use specific phrases that differentiates a counter argument paragraph from a refute paragraph.
5. In general, your thesis does not need information about the counter argument. Ultimately, the counter argument is going to prove your thesis once it is refuted. Therefore, it is already related to your argument.

CHAPTER 14 ACTIVITIES

This style of writing takes practice. Below are some topics that might help you see how to structure an argument essay. Be sure to research both sides of the argument. Also, if it helps, when you brainstorm, be sure to focus your argument. For example, number 1 says "schools." If it helps your essay, you can choose what "school" means, like college or high school.

1. Should schools mandate drug testing?

2. Should everyone go to college?

3. Should there be censorship in the entertainment industry?

4. Should high school students be required to wear uniforms?

5. Should animals be given the same rights as humans?

6. Should fraternities and sororities be part of college life?

7. Should businesses be forced to meet a hiring quota?

8. Are video games good or bad for children?

9. Is the prison system in America effective?

10. Should illegal immigrants have rights in America?

Name: _____   Date: _____

Brainstorm

_____

_____

_____

_____

_____

_____

_____

_____

_____

_____

_____

_____

_____

_____

_____

_____

_____

_____

_____

_____

_____

_____

268

Name: _____   Date: _____

Thesis

_____

_____

_____

_____

_____

_____

_____

_____

_____

_____

_____

_____

_____

_____

_____

_____

_____

Name: _____   Date: _____

Support

_____

_____

_____

_____

_____

_____

_____

_____

_____

_____

_____

_____

_____

_____

_____

_____

_____

_____

The following student sample, written by Alma Colin, is a response to the writing prompt from this chapter's activity, "Should high school students be required to wear uniforms?" This is another controversial and hotly debated topic. Alma takes a stand by arguing that students should be allowed to express themselves and wear whatever they want. Notice how Alma proves her thesis by having each supporting paragraph connect back to that thesis. Also, notice how Alma offers a counter argument (a very common one) in order to strengthen her essay. Does refuting this counter argument make her essay more persuasive? Do you agree or disagree? You can even use Alma's essay to write your own response to this topic in this chapter.

Colin 1

Alma Colin

English 101

14 Nov. 2009

Let Them Wear Clothes!

High school is the beginning of a new adventure for students. It is when many begin to identify who they are. They also begin to explore and find what they want for their future. Students begin to express themselves through many different ways, including the way they want to dress. For many years prior, students were obligated to wear uniform due to many reasons. Although many argue that it is better for high school students to wear a uniform, students should not be required to wear school uniforms. High school students should not be deprived from expressing their individuality and also be forced to purchase them as an additional school expense.

Colin 2

Many people remember their school years as the most memorable. Students remember how they enjoyed matching clothes with friends and even trying new styles once in a while. Many students begin to identify themselves with their friends through the liberty of wearing their favorite clothes. For example, many groups of friends enjoy wearing the same styles of clothing, representing things they like, such as "rock and roll." Females, especially, love to match colors and hair styles that go with them. The popular crowds of friends enjoy looking fashionably fresh wearing the light colors. There are other groups of students who enjoy the rock music and enjoy dressing with darker colors and distinct hair styles. Allowing high school students to dress the way they want to help these young individuals experiment with new things. Interestingly, many students change their style of clothing more than once by observing others and discovering new ideas. In addition to this, "Controlling the socialization process could harm the student as an adult, as they are not prepared for the real world, where they will indeed by judged by their appearances" (Chen). Giving students the freedom to dress with the clothes they like also gives them the opportunity to build more confidence and they are able to become young, independent adults. By requiring uniforms in high school, students would not be given the opportunity of learning or trying something new.

School districts can sometimes not understand the economic conflicts that a uniform can cause at a student's home. They do not realize that uniforms can be very expensive and that there are families that cannot afford them. For example, there have been occasions where students have only one or two uniforms that they use throughout the entire school year. Families with low income often have their child absent if those uniforms were to be ruined. Sometimes, when a student has no financial support, they "find themselves with no other option but to wear less-than pristine school uniforms, which could prompt the very social ostracism school uniforms were ostensibly designed to prevent" (Pollick). The amount of families with low incomes is rapidly increasing, especially during the current recession. Many are unemployed and try their best to provide food and shelter for their children and it often complicates their economical problem more when schools demand uniforms for students. If students are allowed to continue to use their regular clothes, they would be able to use the clothes they already own and not have to go out to purchase anything extra. If they needed to purchase clothing, many would be able to find skirts, jeans, or shirts for a very low cost. While asking a high school student how much she spends on one pair of jeans and a shirt, Jenny Clark replies, "I was able to find my blue jeans and this awesome shirt for about $25 at a fashion store. It doesn't come from an expensive department store but I still look great and many people compliment the way I look." There are many places where good quality clothes are sold without having to spend too much money. Uniforms, on the other hand, are not sold everywhere and in most places, such as JC Penny, sell uniform pants for about $24 and plain white uniform shirts for about $15, which would end up costing a lot more than regular clothes. Saving parents money with the economy at the moment, helps them use the extra money to pay for more important things such as groceries or even rent.

Many high school students enjoy being involved in extracurricular activities, such as clubs or sports. Students, who are fortunate and attend schools that do not require uniforms, are able to join these extracurricular activities without having to worry about financial problems. Many can use their allowances to slowly pay for any extra fees that the club or sport may need. Many are already paying for extra fees such as transportation, ASB, or sport uniform fees. It is unfair that due to an additional expense, such as a daily school uniform, it closes the doors to being involved in other activities that students may be interested in. It is a relief for parents to know that they do not need to spend additional money to pay for school uniforms that are often expensive. In addition to this, "wearing a uniform is not good preparation for working. Only a few jobs require uniforms, and many of these jobs are

low-paid jobs—not what we want our young people to aim for" (Endersby).
Most of the well-paid jobs that are offered that require uniforms are those in
the medical field. Many of these uniforms are offered in different styles and
colors, which still allow for workers to express their individuality.

However, many argue that high school students will benefit from
wearing uniforms. They say that uniforms will eliminate the problems between
social classes. It is also said that when students wear regular clothes, many are
put down by the rich children who are showing off their expensive clothing.
Those who come from wealthy backgrounds often buy and wear expensive
brand name clothing, causing conflict between the upper and middle class,
even within the school. As written by Grace Chen, by using uniforms "the peer
pressures of stylish dressing with the 'best' brands are alleviated, and students
can focus more upon their schoolwork, rather than social appearances." Many
times, the middle class students are blamed for missing objects such as
expensive sweaters. Instructors believe that by eliminating the clothing factor
and continuing the usage of uniforms, everything in the school will remain
peaceful. On the contrary, what many instructors do not understand is that
using a uniform has not prevented any conflicts between social classes.

Students have always found a way to express who they are and where
they belong in society. Using uniforms only masks the problems between the

Colin 6

classes. Until now, many students have been discriminated against because they might be more economically "unstable." Rich students are still able to show off their social status through even the simplest accessory they own. For example, the students that are wealthy and that are expected to wear uniforms still flaunt their shoes, their backpacks, and even their jewelry. If they notice that another child owns a "generic" backpack, that student might be bullied on a daily basis. Also, if low income parents are not able to afford expensive shoes, like Nike, the parent might buy a pair of cheap shoes from Payless, which is often considered embarrassing for many students who are picked on because they are not wealthy. Students are always aware of the newest trends and a school uniform will not change or improve the situations between social classes.

Arguments about the usage of uniforms in high school will continue for a long period of time. However, uniforms should not be required for students. Problems in social classes will always exist, including outside of school. Wearing uniforms will definitely not terminate the problem, and instructors, as well as parents, should approach that conflict in a different manner. Students that are not obligated to wear uniforms learn and experiment with different styles of clothing. Students with low incomes are given the opportunity to use the extra money to be able to participate in other

Colin 7

activities that they enjoy, such as sports or music. Parents would not have to

worry about purchasing uniforms annually if students were allowed to use the

wardrobe they already own at home. Students are full of amazing creations

and self-expressions ready to bloom and they should not be suppressed by the

conformity brought by a uniform.

Colin 8

Works Cited

Chen, Grace. "Public School Uniforms: The Pros and Cons for Your Child."

 Review Public School. Public School Review LLC. 23 Apr. 2008. Web.

 6 Nov. 2009.

Clark, Jenny. Personal Interview. 8 Nov. 2009.

Endersby, Alastair. "School Uniform (Junior)." *IDEA.* IDEA.inc. 27 Apr. 2006.

 Web. 6 Nov. 2009.

Pollick, Michael. "What are the Pros and Cons of Requiring School

 Uniforms?" *Conjecture Corporation.* 2009. Web. 6 Nov. 2009.

The following student sample, written by Armando Palomares-flores, is a response to the writing prompt "Violence in Television." This particular prompt was not a question, so the student needed to develop his own question in order to create his own argument. As you read, be sure to pay attention to the thesis. What kind of claim is being made? Also, notice how this essay follows the argument—counter argument—refute the counter argument pattern.

Palomares-flores, Armando

English 101

November 19, 2008

Violence in Television

The website of the World Health Organization states, "Each year, over 1.6 million people worldwide lose their lives to violence. Violence is among the leading causes of death for people aged 15–44 years worldwide . . ." ("Violence"). This is a truly sad situation that affects our society. Crime and violence are increasing day by day at an alarming speed. Unfortunately, young people are the most affected group. A variety of causes contribute to this phenomenon including lack of education, biological and psychological issues. While TV violence is not the only cause of aggressive or violent behavior, it is clearly a significant factor. For this reason, TV shows that expose violence should be banned from being aired. By doing this, violence among youngsters would be reduced, benefiting society as a whole.

Young people become more aggressive due to their exposure to violence in television programs. People at a young age do not know the difference between what is good and proper and what is not. They tend to imitate what they see in TV shows, thinking that it is okay to do it, even if it is just a funny cartoon. For example, a kindergarten kid would think that saying a bad word in class is fine because he heard it in TV, or worse, he might hurt his classmates following the same example. Cases like this happen all the time in all levels of school. A joint statement signed by representatives from six of the nation's top public health organizations, including the American Academy of Pediatrics, the American Psychological Association, and the American Medical Association indicates:

> Well over 1000 studies . . . point overwhelmingly to a causal connection between media violence and aggressive behavior in some children. The conclusion of the public health community, based on over 30 years of research, is that viewing entertainment violence can lead to increases in aggressive attitudes, values and behavior, particularly in children. ("TV Bloodbath: Violence on Prime Time Broadcast TV")

It is clear that television affects children, increasing their aggressive attitudes. Moreover, police and detective shows, violent cartoons, wrestling and other

TV programs are popular among young people. These TV shows introduce them to the use of guns, killing, drugs, blood, aggressiveness, hate, sex, and bitter rivalry. It is alarming that teens are being affected by the violence of television, making them more aggressive.

Due to violence in television, children become immune to the horror of violence and might accept it as a way to solve problems. The extensive viewing of television violence makes the viewer comfortable with it, especially kids. This situation is a problem because it leads to loss of innocence at an early age, making teens prone to commit, or be part of, crimes without any consequences. Moreover, due to the familiarization of young people with violence, they see the violence as a way to solve problems encountered in life. For instance, adolescents prefer to solve their differences with others by fighting or using aggressive behaviors towards them instead of talking about the issue. Paige Egan indicates, "Fifteen year old Kip Kinkel, a smart, popular if sullen boy from a prosperous two career family murdered his parents, slept well in his own bed, then, toting weapons worthy of an Iraqi terrorist in his back pack, mowed down 24 of his fellow students" (Egan). It is obvious that this teenager did not hesitate to commit this horrible crime and had previous knowledge of how to use firearms. Perhaps, if he had not followed the example witnessed on TV and communicated to his parents some of the issues affecting him, this tragedy could have been prevented. Violence in TV does affect youngsters, giving them the incentive to react with violent acts and ultimately making them prone to use violence to solve their problems.

The increase of violence among young people affects society in negative ways. TV exposes children to different violent situations creating fear in them and changing the way they see life. Because of this, they are prone to distrust other people. In an Internet article, Kerby Anderson says, ". . . people who watch a lot of TV see the real world as more dangerous and frightening than those who watch very little. Heavy viewers are less trustful of their fellow citizens and more fearful of the real world" (Anderson). Social development is affected by situations like this. Moreover, it has been proven that children that spend large amounts of time watching violent TV shows are prone to develop aggressive behaviors as they grow up. This is especially true in men. For example, in a study from the University of Michigan, research shows:

> . . . that men who were high TV-violence viewers as children were significantly more likely to have pushed, grabbed or shoved their spouses, to have responded to an insult by shoving a person, to have been convicted of a crime and to have committed a moving traffic violation. (Kaufman)

The more time children spend watching TV shows that contain violence the more chances are that they will become aggressive people in the future. This problem will lead to more violence and crime in our society. There is no doubt that society is affected by violence created by the violent TV programs.

It is argued by some people that there are two ways to help parents prevent children from watching violent TV shows. The first one is the V chip, which is intended to block certain television programs. Kevin Szaflik says, "The chip would allow parents to prevent a television program from being seen in their homes if a rating system determined that it had a high level of violent or sexually explicit content" (Szaflik). This chip would help parents to decide what kind of programs their children are able to watch in every TV they own. The second one is the use of the Rating System. This system was developed to inform parents about the content of the show, helping them to decide whether the program is secure for their children to watch. These include the common ratings we see today, such as TV-PG, which is parental guidance suggested and TV-MA, which is for mature audiences only. In terms of these ratings, Szaflik states, "The ratings would be made by the producers and distributors of shows, and would be printed in newspaper TV listings so parents could use them as a guide for shielding their kids from rough stuff on the tube." These ratings would give parents more control and could make a

Palomares-flores 6

difference in the programming that children are allowed to watch. Clearly, these two methods could make the task of preventing young people from being exposed to violence easier.

However, the previously mentioned methods have several flaws that make them pointless. Even though the V chip has a 4 digit password protection to avoid children from changing the settings, it is easy to reset and can be done by anyone with access to the TV's manual or the Internet. Moreover, the fact that most households own more than one TV set makes it harder for parents to control V chip configurations. For instance, the living room's TV might be set up to block certain content, but the TV in the kitchen or in the parents' room might not have the V chip activated. The rating system is also faulty because it is too general because it has been divided by age groups. It does not tell parents what exactly is going to happen in the TV show. Szaflik states that in a survey released by the Media Studies Center, 79% of the parents polled said they preferred a system that specifies the objectionable content to a general one giving only age limits. Another poll conducted by *US News and World Report* found that 62 percent of parents prefer a system based on content instead of age markers (Szaflik). The rating system does not really help parents to decide whether a TV show is appropriate for their kids or not. Moreover, a parent's cultural and personal background affects what situations they think are appropriate for children to watch. Finally, for these methods to work, constant supervision is needed, which today, is nearly impossible. There is no doubt that none of these methods is suitable to help parents avoid their kids from watching violent television programs. Therefore, the only viable solution is to ban all violent TV programs and violent images from the airwaves.

Young people are greatly affected by the influence of violent TV programming. Violence in TV makes youngsters insensitive to violent acts and more aggressive towards other people. Society is also damaged by this situation. People think that television programs are a reflection of the real world, making them afraid of it and preventing them from trusting other people. It is true that there are some methods to prevent children from watching violent TV shows. However, they have limited effectiveness and are not embraced by society as a solution to the problem. Clearly, the most viable solution to this problem is to ban violent TV programs from being aired, protecting the young children from the violence and protecting the future of our society.

Works Cited

Anderson, Kerby. "Violence In Society." *Leadership U.* Probe Ministries,

    14 July 2002. Web. 18 Nov. 2008.

Egan, Paige. "Lost Innocence, Could Your Child Kill?" *dadmag.com.*

    Dadmag.com LLC, 13 Oct. 2000. Web. 18 Nov. 2008.

Kaufman, Ron. "Filling Their Minds With Death: TV Violence And Children."

    turnoffyourtv.com. Turn Off Your TV, 2004. Web. 18 Nov. 2008.

Szaflik, Kevin. "Violence on TV: The Desensitizing Of America." 24 Nov.

    2004. Web. 18 Nov. 2008. < http://www.ridgenet.org/szaflik/

    tvrating.htm>.

"TV Bloodbath: Violence On Prime Time Broadcast TV." *parentstv.org.*

    Parents Television Council, 2008. Web. 18 Nov. 2008.

"Violence." *World Health Organization.* World Health Organization, 2008.

    Web. 18 Nov. 2008. < http://www.who.int/violence_injury_

    prevention/violence/en/>.

PART 4

Further Information

CHAPTER 15

Formality

Whether or not you realize it, this book has been teaching you how to write *formal* college essays. Professors vary on what they consider to be "formal," but the ideas presented here are generally considered formal. The best way to understand what your teacher wants in an essay is to ask. Once you understand what is necessary to succeed, you will know how to approach an essay.

Some of these ideas and techniques will take time and practice to achieve, but once you do, you will see a difference in your writing. With each essay you write, you should start to see the language and the quality of your writing improve. For example, if a professor requires a five-page essay, you might start to panic and ask yourself, "How do I write such a long essay?" Everything you have done in this book has prepared you to write any type of essay, so you already have all of the tools needed to write five pages. This means that the next time a professor asks for an eight-page essay, or a fifteen-page essay, you will no longer panic. Instead, you will know how to approach your topic, do the necessary research, create a thesis, and write the essay.

How you write, the actual physical words, is completely up to you (there are an infinite number of sentences in the English language). The way you write is your style, and it will be different from other people in your class. This idea of formality, both the physical appearance of your essay and the words written, is an important part of your success. That is why there will be many hints throughout this chapter.

Some of the information you might already know—it is included because students make these mistakes on a regular basis. So even if you read the idea and you laugh it off, just be aware that it is an easy mistake to make. You need to be conscious of these ideas when you proofread because they all affect the formality.

1. In the upper-left corner of your essay, you should put your name. MLA requires that you put your first and last name in the upper-left corner, in that order. However, some professors require that you write your last name first, then your first name. Professors do this because their database lists you by

your last name. This way, everything is consistent and organized. You always need to know what the professor requires so that you properly format your name in the upper-left corner.

2. Here are the other formatting guidelines. These requirements are standard in MLA. Your essay should be typed using Times New Roman font and 12 points in size. Your essay should be double spaced. You need 1″ margins on all sides of your page. Finally, be sure to put page numbers with your last name next to that number in the upper-right corner of every page of your essay.

3. A sentence must have a subject, verb, and noun. There are no exceptions. A standard paragraph must be five or more sentences. There are no exceptions. A "standard essay" is five paragraphs. But with all the things you have learned in this book, your essays can be much longer.

4. In formal writing, you should remove all personal statements. Personal statements are phrases like "I think," "In my opinion," and "I believe." Although you might be tempted to start a sentence this way, you really should avoid doing this. You can think of the personal statement like this: your name is on the essay, so the reader automatically knows the essay is your opinion. Your thesis is your opinion, hence your argument. Writing "I believe" ends up being redundant. It is possible to take any sentence you write in the first person and turn it into third person. For example, if you write, "I believe capital punishment is wrong," you can change that to read, "Capital punishment is wrong." Both express an opinion, but the second sentence is formal. Doing this consistently throughout your essay will give your paper a formal tone. Finally, by removing all personal statements, you will be arguing the information, not your beliefs.

5. In addition to first person, you also want to remove the use of second person. This means you do not want to write "you" as part of your analysis in your paragraphs. This is important for several reasons. First, you do not want to talk to the reader like you are having a conversation. Second, there is a good chance the reader is not the "you" you are referring to. For example, try to avoid writing like this: "Living in a rural area means that you have to get up early and you have to milk the cows." In this case, the reader might not live in a rural area, which means that person is not getting up early to milk cows. Instead of writing using the second person, switch to third person with phrases like "people," "individuals," or "one." For example, this sentence reads better: "Some people that live in rural areas must wake up early and milk the cows." Now you have written a strong sentence.

6. Formal writing means no contractions. You may not realize this, but there is a verb found in many contractions, and students often create a verb tense error because of the contraction. You need to remove them from your writing by writing the words as they would normally appear. Many word processing programs can be set to detect contractions and fix them for you. For example, words such as "don't" should be written as "do not" and "haven't" should be written as "have not." Remember, "can't" becomes "cannot," which is one word.

7. Formal writing means that you need to avoid using slang, which is the informal language consisting of words and expressions that are not considered appropriate in formal writing. The use of slang falls into many categories, but in an essay, it means to avoid foul language, jargon (confused, unintelligible language), colloquialisms (a local or regional dialect expression), and anything that directly affects the tone of your essay. The best way to look at it is like this: in general, you should not write the way you talk. There are too many slang expressions to list. Here is a very common mistake that can be labeled as slang. Some students write, "Same can be said. . . ." It is missing a word and needs to be written as "The same can be said . . ."

8. In formal writing, you should never use short hand. We live in a modern world with e-mail and text messaging—as a writer, you need to learn the difference between that kind of informal writing and a formal essay. This means you should never shorten a word or phrase as you would in an electronic communication. For example, students often write "u" when they really mean "you." And just because a street sign says "thru" does not mean it is spelled correctly. The word is spelled "through."

9. When referencing something that is current, all you need to write is the word "today." Avoid getting creative with this reference—students often make the mistake of writing "now a days" or "these days" when all they really mean is "today."

10. In fact, keeping things simple leads to clarity. A good formal essay is clear in its ability to communicate arguments and information. If you can take a straight approach to what you need to say, do it. Avoid wordiness.

11. You should also learn to spot common mistakes between words that sound the same but are spelled differently. For example, you need to learn the difference between "there" "their," and "they're" (the last one should not be used because you would not use a contraction, so you would write "they are"). Similar examples include "weather" and "whether"; "two," "too," and "to"; and "affect" and "effect."

12. Proofreading is very important! It is also a very hard skill to master. Most people cannot proofread their own work. This is because as you read, you know what you meant to say and what words belong where, making it very easy to miss a mistake. In fact, read the sentences that follow.

"Aoccdrnig to a rscheearch at Cmabrigde Uinervtisy, it deosn't mttaer in waht oredr the ltteers in a wrod are, the olny iprmoetnt tihng is taht the frist and lsat ltteer be at the rghit pclae. The rset can be a toatl mses and you can sitll raed it wouthit a porbelm. Tihs is bcuseae the huamn mnid deos not raed ervey lteter by istlef, but the wrod as a wlohe."

The fact that you can read these sentences shows how easy it is to overlook errors you make in your own writing. Your mind will see what it knows should be there even if the word is wrong.

Now, try this:

Count the number of "F's" in the following text:

Finished files are the result of years of scientific study combined with the experience of years.

How many did you find? You probably counted three "F's," right?

Now you know why proofreading is so hard! However, there is an easy solution. Find a classmate, friend, coworker, or family member whom you trust to proofread your essay. Also, most colleges have writing centers that can help you proofread your essay. In other words, the final version of your essay that you turn in to your professor should be as free from errors as possible. If these do not work for you, try reading your essay out loud. You will be amazed at how many errors you find.

There are actually six "F's." This is because the human brain cannot process "of" as a word containing individual letters. Our brain sees the word "of" as one word; hence, we overlook the letter "f." So if you counted all six on the first try, you are a genius. Three is what most people count. Once again, this shows that proofreading can be difficult.

There are many things to consider in this chapter, all of which are designed to help you write a formal essay. But not just any formal essay—the best one *you* can write. The goal is to take **pride** in your work. What you turn in to your professor should be as formal, clean, and as free from errors as possible. That means if you print a page and the text is hard to read, print it again. It means proofreading to find the obvious mistakes. It means using a formal tone to communicate ideas and arguments (nobody wants to read a melodramatic essay). If you take pride in your words, thoughts, arguments, and the appearance of your final essay, you will see the results you want.

CHAPTER 16

Sentence Meaning

The English language is not easy to master, especially when trying to write an essay that clearly communicates your argument. There are many grammatical rules to learn, as well as mastering sentence structure. This chapter is not about the rules of grammar nor is it going to rely on the technical definitions of grammar and sentence structure. Instead, this chapter is going to focus on the "meaning" of a sentence. In other words, by looking at some of the common issues that students face when writing, we will see how sentences do not always mean what the writer intended. This problem occurs when a sentence in your essay is not properly constructed.

Sentence meaning is difficult to detect because most people proofread for spelling and grammar errors. Finding sentence meaning errors requires a different kind of proofreading skill—you have to read each sentence slowly, as if that sentence is communicating a single cohesive idea. Then, you need to proofread by reading the other sentences around it to make sure everything makes sense. After reading this chapter, I hope you become more aware of these types of errors and you begin looking for them in your own assignments.

Some of these sentences, all written by real students, might sound humorous to you—if the sentence makes you laugh, you are recognizing why sentence meaning is so important. Your goal should always be to write a sentence that clearly states your argument, one that is straightforward and logical.

As you read each type of sentence meaning error and the corresponding examples, you should be thinking about two things: what is wrong with the sentence and what is needed to correct the problem?

1) Incomplete Thoughts

This error occurs when a sentence ends abruptly. When the sentence ends abruptly, the reader is left questioning the meaning of the sentence. Incomplete thoughts also occur when a writer uses words that are vague, or ambiguous, which makes the sentence unclear. Incomplete thoughts are easy to fix—be specific. In each example, how would you re-write the sentence to make it clearer?

"Everyday, there are people who drink coffee assuming that they will get better."

"In order to solve the major topic of homelessness in our country, we must resolve the enormous contributions of the subtopics it attains."

"Although determination improves a goal, actual ability is critical in the following through of an idea."

2) Clichés

A cliché is a trite or overused expression or idea. In academic and formal writing, it is more important to write what you mean rather than relying on the cliché to say it for you. In addition, a cliché implies that you are using more than just a common phrase—you can also be making an unusual metaphor which affects the meaning of your sentence. This kind of writing can be jarring for the reader. In each example, I know you will understand the sentence, but what can be done to make it more formal and acceptable for academic writing?

"In spite of these rosy feelings that arise, things are not as bright as they seem."

"Thus, they rid the entire country of even bigger issues caused by monsters on four wheels."

"When using crystal meth, users are getting more than just a simple high; they will be getting a combination of stuff that can make the prettiest of models look ugly."

3) Unintentionally False

This occurs when the author writes something that ends up being false. It happens because of the words chosen to construct the sentence or because of the location of the words in the sentence reveals an idea that cannot be true. Sometimes a sentence becomes unintentionally false because the author does not know how to say what he/she means. Although the sentence might be grammatically correct, the sentence's meaning is unclear. As you read these examples, can you detect what makes each one false? How would you fix each example?

"Even if a patient is known to not be able to survive, they should be given the choice to survive even if they are not conscious."

"It is hard to drive down the street without seeing a fast food restaurant, and wanting to get a quick bite."

"Some people tend to believe that several types of illness can spread through the world because of experiences, visualization, or stats. In brief, human activity can affect the human health because scientists believe that statistics say it all."

4) Avoid Redundancy

Redundancy occurs when a word or phrase is used multiple times within the sentence. It can be a simple word or a complex phrase—either way, you will recognize the redundancy in the examples below. In addition, redundancy can happen between multiple sentences. If this happens to you, try re-writing your sentences using other words (a thesaurus might help) or write a simpler sentence in order to remove unnecessary words. How would you fix these sentences?

"These kinds of war seem to justify their acts of war, and sounds like a war for a great cause. At the same time, they suggest that great casualties were inevitable for a great cause."

"As it is, the adults that control the money, the focus has been on obesity in adults. As a result, research into obesity is primarily aimed at adults."

"Many uneducated citizens, who have never attended school, continue to vote for bond measures that are expected to improve schools."

5) Avoid Wordiness

Some students like to embellish their sentences with extra words—the extra words make their sentences longer and in effect, make the essay longer. However, your writing should always be clear and to the point. This means getting rid of wordy sentences. Write exactly what you mean to say. In the examples below, see if you understand what the author is trying to say and how the same thing can be said in a much shorter, clearer sentence.

"It is a very lucid and convincing piece in which I have found great relation and can totally agree with especially due to recent events instigated by the actions of our former American leader(s) in the fragile era of diplomacy."

"In my first example of why I disagree with saving our endangered species, I would like to use a famous line introduced to the world through his book *On the Origin of Species*."

"A mindset based on a mathematical model best suits the making of decisions that affect a company's future business relations with other companies."

6) **Wrong Analysis**

If you recall our discussion of paragraph development in an earlier chapter, any direct quote or example used as support should be analyzed within the paragraph. However, the analysis you write must be related to the support. In other words, you cannot conclude something different than what the support states. If you do, you have created the wrong analysis error. In this example, carefully read what PETA says about AIDS. Then, read what the student thinks PETA said, and you will see how they are completely unrelated.

"The Second Amendment to the Constitution states, 'a well-regulated militia being necessary to the security of a free state, the right of the people to keep and bear arms shall not be infringed.' It is obvious from this, that everyone has a right to carry a weapon and use it for self defense."

"An article in today's paper states that for the first time since 1975 there will be no COLA (cost of living adjustment) for those receiving Social Security. Clearly, Obama's reckless spending is putting a strain on the Federal budget."

"PETA submits for consideration that 'population studies demonstrated the mechanism of the transmission of AIDS and other infectious diseases and also showed how these diseases can be prevented.' With this knowledge in hand, it is then possible to let those infected with AIDS die out, thus letting them take the disease with them, all without coming to harm another animal."

7) **Faulty Comparison**

Faulty comparison is a common fallacy that occurs in Compare/Contrast essays, but it is often difficult to detect. Faulty comparison occurs when you try to compare two things that cannot be compared, usually because they are unrelated or have elements that make the two things drastically different. Although most things can be contrasted, the idea that two things have something in common needs to be fully justified. For example:

"Doctors and lawyers are not only permitted to consult texts, but are expected to. Therefore, students should be allowed to consult texts during examinations."

"The human body, as it grows older, becomes less effective and it eventually dies. Thus, it is reasonable to assume that political bodies, as they grow older, will become less and less effective, and that they also will eventually die."

"I honestly believe that if criminals and phobic people have been known to fix their way of thinking, then so can dogs with a little effort...in any type of psychology be it human or dog psychology, when someone is fulfilled emotionally and naturally, then they are happy, thus balanced and less troublesome."

The problem with the last one is that the author is comparing criminals (of any kind, violent or otherwise), phobic people (who have a fear of something, even something as common as a fear of spiders), and dog psychology. Those three things cannot and should not be compared this way. Now that the sentence has been broken down this way, do you see the faulty comparison fallacy?

CHAPTER 17

The In-Class Essay

In-class essays are different than the essays you write at home. In-class essays are usually written with added pressure—*time*. A timed essay requires different approaches and different techniques in order to achieve the highest grade possible.

However, everything you have learned in this book still applies. That means you want to follow the basic strategies of writing an essay, including organization, paragraph development, and formality. Those things do not change because you are in a classroom.

Here are a few hints to help ease the pressure of a timed essay:

1. Be prepared! If the professor tells you what might be on the test, study all those "might-be's" so you can answer any question.

2. When you get the test, read all the questions before choosing one. Then, once you know the essay you are going to write, take a few minutes to brainstorm. Do a quick cluster or an outline so you know how you will approach the essay. It takes about ten minutes to brainstorm and organize your thoughts, so balance your time based on how long you are given for the test.

3. An in-class essay is graded mainly on organization and communication of ideas and arguments. That is why brainstorming and preparing to answer the question is so important. You need a strong thesis to unite your essay and show that you understand the topic. Again, this is where strong paragraphs, organized around a focused argument, are important. If you can communicate your thoughts clearly during a timed test, you will usually score high.

4. In addition, most professors do not take off as many points for spelling and grammatical errors. For example, a misspelled word does not hurt your grade as much as the same misspelled word at home. But you MUST follow all the same rules of formality required for a sentence. If you suddenly write improper sentences, that will affect your grade. In other words, you still need to use the basic rules of grammar correctly throughout a timed test. If you find this to be a problem, try writing simple sentences that communicate ideas rather than complex sentences that tend to be grammatically incorrect.

5. Another important element of the essay to consider is based on the kind of support you use. At home, you can add support and verify information by doing research and using quotes. However, you cannot do this during a timed test. Even though you need support for your arguments, the support does not need to be *as* specific. For example, if you are talking about a certain number of people in a survey, you can say "about half of the people . . ." Or, you may need to rely on a more descriptive example to make your point. Whatever you do, do not make up information. Your support still needs to be accurate.

6. We have discussed many different types of essays. Each type has structures and methods designed to help you organize an essay. Do not invent a new method during a test. Rely on the things you have learned about those types of essays. If the question asks to compare two ideas, you should immediately rely on what you learned about the comparison/contrast essay.

7. Do not think because you know everything about a topic that you need to write everything you know. Watch out for this trap because students do this often. You must answer the question asked on the test. All the other information you add that has no relevance to the topic might hurt your score. In other words, it is quality and accuracy of the answer that scores higher than quantity.

8. Always write neatly. Since a professor has to read your handwriting, write the essay as clearly as possible, so you do not lose points because something is not legible.

9. Always go back and check your work. Give yourself time to proofread your essay to find careless errors, spelling and grammar errors, and ideas that are not connected.

10. Finally, the most important thing to understand about a timed test is how to allocate your time based on your writing skills. The only way to do this is to practice, so that when the time comes to take an actual test, you are prepared. For example, if you have a two hour test, try to balance your time so that you can maximize the amount of time you spend writing. Read the questions and brainstorm the topic you want to write about. Give yourself about ten minutes for this. Then begin writing and give yourself about ten minutes at the end to proofread the entire essay. Out of two hours, this would give you about one hour and forty minutes of actual writing, keeping in mind that you start and stop often, get distracted, or change your brainstorm to include a new idea. This would be a good recommendation for a timed essay.

Writing timed, in-class essays, can cause stress, but hopefully the advice given here lessens that stress. Learning to put this advice into action takes practice, and if you practice, you will improve your in-class writing skills.

CHAPTER 17 ACTIVITIES

Here is a chance to practice. Be sure to follow the instructions!

Directions: In a well-organized and well-argued essay, choose one of the topics to express your views in a formal tone. Remember to set your parameters, provide examples, and use whichever essay method(s) needed to support your arguments. Also, be sure to proofread carefully, write clearly, and stay on-topic. The professor will set the time limit.

1. Should colleges allow corporate advertising in the form of banners and fliers in the classroom?

2. Should we modify the current structure for movie ratings? In regards to the G, PG, PG-13, R ratings, do they work, should we change them, and how should they be enforced?

3. Should law enforcement be allowed to issue tickets via the mail, even if they did not give you a ticket in person?

Name: _____   Date: _____

Brainstorm

_____

_____

_____

_____

_____

_____

_____

_____

_____

_____

_____

_____

_____

_____

_____

_____

_____

_____

Name: _____   Date: _____

Thesis

_____

_____

_____

_____

_____

_____

_____

_____

_____

_____

_____

_____

_____

_____

_____

_____

_____

Name: _____   Date: _____

Support

_____

_____

_____

_____

_____

_____

_____

_____

_____

_____

_____

_____

_____

_____

_____

_____

PART 5

Additional Student Essays

Additional Student Samples

The following student sample, written by Joseph Sosta, is a response to the writing prompt "censorship in the media." This particular prompt was not a question, so the student needed to develop his own question in order to create his own argument. As you read, be sure to pay attention to the thesis. What kind of claim is being made? How is support used throughout the essay? Is the author's argument consistent? What kinds of essay strategies can you spot in this essay?

Joseph Sosta

English 1A

Responsibility for the Censorship of Violent Television Content

During the halftime show of Super Bowl XXXVIII in February of 2004, about 20 percent of American children were exposed to a glimpse of Janet Jackson's bare breast that lasted for several seconds. In response to this, more than half a million complaints from viewers were filed and over $500,000 in fines were levied by the Federal Communications Commission (FCC) against the television stations that aired the broadcast (Ahrens and De Moraes). That same year, thousands of movies, television shows, and newscasts also aired and exposed countless American children to innumerable scenes of violence, yet no fines were levied against the violent content. This is because the FCC's regulations are only concerned with limiting the broadcast of obscene or indecent content, not violent content. In spite of research that has shown that violent television has a negative and immediate effect on the children who view it, little change has come in the laws governing how violent programming is regulated. Because of the fact that the FCC, as a government agency, is beholden to the American public, the responsibility to change regulatory policy with specific regard toward violent programming rests squarely in the hands of the American public. While the FCC helped to put in place a system of TV show ratings as well as mandating the inclusion of a piece of technology in television sets which can use those ratings to block programming, it is only through proactive behavior that parents are able to censor what their children can watch. Since greater changes in the regulatory policies of the FCC seem unlikely, it lies in the hands of parents to continue to censor the television their children watch as well as to educate their children about the seriousness of the violence being shown on TV. At the same time, the American public must continue to push for more effective regulation of violent content on television.

According to the FCC website, the FCC is a government agency that was formed as a result of the Communications Act of 1934 and is responsible for regulating television broadcasts ("About the FCC"). The FCC has the responsibility of enforcing federal regulations that prohibit the airing of obscene programming as well as limit the times during which it is acceptable to air indecent programming or programming that contains profane language. Obscene material (generally regarded as hardcore pornography) may not be broadcast at any time since the Supreme Court has ruled that the First Amendment does not protect it. Indecent or profane material can be aired but at times of day when children would be less likely to view it, such as late at night. The entry for Television Regulation in the *Encyclopedia of Children, Adolescents, and the Media* states:

> The FCC defines *indecency* as 'language or material that depicts or describes, in terms patently offensive as measured by contemporary community standards for the broadcast medium, sexual or excretory activities or organs.' *Profanity* is defined as 'certain of those personally reviling epithets naturally tending to provoke violent resentment or denoting language so grossly offensive to members of the public who actually hear it as to amount to a nuisance.' (McGregor)

Dow Lohnes PLLC expands upon this by stating that a broadcast is not considered to be indecent when it portrays violent, but not sexual programming ("FCC Regulation" 4). The FCC enforces the laws regarding obscenity, indecency, and profanity based upon complaints filed by the public. Public complaints about violent content in a broadcast would not be acted upon because, as stated on the "Obscenity, Indecency, and Profanity - Frequently Asked Questions" page of the FCC website, "The FCC does not currently regulate the broadcast of violent programming" ("Obscenity"). In response to the Telecommunications Act of 1996, the broadcasting industry set up a ratings system known as "TV Parental Guidelines" that aims to rate programming based on "sexual [content], violent [content], or other material parents may deem inappropriate" ("FCC V-Chip"). The FCC has adopted rules that require modern television sets to be capable of blocking TV programming based upon its rating. However, in spite of both of these advances, there are still no policies prohibiting or limiting the airing of violent content.

According to the article "Television Violence and Its Effect on Young Children" by Betty J. Simmons, Kelly Stalsworth, and Heather Wentzel, studies on the effect of television programming on young children have been conducted since the early 1950s. Studies from 1952 to 1967 focused on the content of programming, while studies done in the late 1960s and early 1970s turned toward examining the effects of violence on viewers. The findings in the later studies concluded that there was a direct relationship between violent programming and violent behavior in children (Simmons et al. 149). A study by Berkowitz in 1962 came to the conclusion that exposure to violent programming led to a rise in aggressive behavior in children, especially if they believed the violent behavior on television was justified (Simmons et al. 150). In light of such a direct connection being made between violent content and violent or negative behavior in children, one would hope that the FCC would seek to amend the regulatory policies to better protect children from such an obviously harmful form of entertainment. That assumption is made all that much more reasonable because of how strictly the FCC regulates sexually

related content. While the FCC did help establish a ratings system for

television programming that is based both on its sexual content as well as its

violent content, it never established regulations or fines that outright prohibit

violent content from airing at any time of day (as it has done with sexual

content). What the FCC did do is require that all television sets made after

January 1, 2000 be built with features that can block the display of

programming based upon its rating ("FCC V-Chip"). While this was a

significant step in the right direction, it ultimately still leaves the responsibility

for blocking programming of a violent nature in the hands of parents.

  With the V-Chip technology now built into all new television sets,

parents have a means, limited though it may be, to block some or all violent

programming. According to Joanne Cantor's entry on the V-Chip in the

Encyclopedia of Communications and Information, the V-Chip works by

reading the program rating that is broadcast with a show, and either blocking

or allowing it to be displayed, dependant upon how it is set up at the time

(Cantor). Unfortunately for even pro-active parents, the V-Chip technology is

an imperfect system. One of the biggest limitations is the voluntary nature of

the rating system itself. Because rating a program is not mandatory, a

television station can pick and choose which programs to rate. Some programming, such as newscasts and sporting events, is generally unrated,

even on stations that broadcast ratings for most other programming. Parents can

simply block all unrated content, but then they run the risk of also blocking

informative or educational programming. Another pitfall, specific to sporting

events and newscasts, is that while both could contain beneficial programming

for children, both are also quite likely to carry violent imagery (especially in a

time of ongoing war). Art Hilgart states in an article for the *Humanist* that, "the

problem with ratings and censorship, in addition to conflicting with the pesky

Constitution, is that brains are never part of the equation—a single formula

applies to Fellini, Bergman, and cheap skin flicks." The ratings system tries to

function without any active thought. It sets up an arbitrary, broad, and

generalized set of rules upon which programming is rated.

Another flaw in the ratings system used by the V-Chip, is that violence

can be categorized as "comedic violence" or "fantasy violence" which fall

under a less severe rating ("FCC V-chip"). While cartoon violence, which

often falls under the category of comedic violence, is generally unrealistic, it

still has the potential for being imitated by children. The tendency of children

to mimic what they see portrayed even in something as innocent as a cartoon

could ultimately lead to rather aggressive behavior. The ratings system is setup

in such a way that it makes certain forms of violence more acceptable than others. There is no ideal setting for the v-Chip technology. Parents constantly have to activate, deactivate, and change the settings regarding what is being blocked in order to ensure that the programming that their children can watch is appropriate. Parents would benefit more from further reform to the television ratings system and regulations that dictate that all programming adhere to the ratings system so that programs might more accurately be blocked by the V-Chip.

The nature of the FCC is such that most regulatory action it takes is as a result of public complaints. The fines levied against television stations for the broadcast of Janet Jackson's exposed breast were as high as they were simply because of the volume of complaints received by the FCC. In 2006, the FCC resolved "more than 300,000 complaints" made against approximately 50 different programs that had been broadcast over a three-year period ("FCC Regulation" 1). All of those complaints originated with private citizens. In light of such a monumental level of influence held over the FCC by the American public, it should then also fall to that same public to push for changes in the regulations governing the FCC. While parents would still have to monitor what their children are watching on television, regulatory changes would allow for an added level of control over the broadcasting of violent programming (much as the regulation concerning sexually charged material does). Current laws state that indecent programming can only be aired later in the evening in an effort to keep children from being exposed to sexually charged content, but there are no such regulations for violent content. By changing the laws so that violent programming could only air in the evenings, for example, parents would not have to constantly monitor what their children are able to watch during the day. In augmenting the scope of the regulatory policies it would also make it so that complaints to the FCC about violent programming could be enforced with warnings and fines. Under the current regulations, complaints regarding violent programming will not result in a fine, as there are no laws banning or limiting the broadcast of violent content. If the current definitions of obscene, indecent, or profane programming were expanded so that they included violent content as well, it would easily remedy this issue. By changing the regulations enforced by the FCC, parents would gain a more effective means to ensure that programming which would be broadcast when children are most likely to view it was of a more suitable nature.

Current FCC regulations afford parents a significant amount of help from the FCC with regard to indecent or profane programming. Parents do not, however, have an effective means by which to control or remove violent programming from television at this time. Only by actively and constantly monitoring the ratings and content of television programs can parents hope to stop the torrent of violent programming that children are exposed to. While the FCC has made some advances (such as requiring technology like the v-Chip in televisions, or the creation of a television ratings system) it still has yet to put any regulation in place that would allow it to fine networks for airing violent content of any sort. This is even in light of all research that has shown violent television to have a negative influence in the behavior of children. In an effort to combat the amount of violent programming on television, Congress passed the Telecommunications Act of 1996, which helped to set up the current television ratings system. Unfortunately, little change has come about because of this, as the FCC still does not regulate violent programming. Ultimately, the responsibility of monitoring what children watch on television will continue to fall completely on parents until the policies of the FCC are changed in such a way as to better protect children from inappropriate content, be it violent or sexually charged. Since the American public can so readily call the FCC to action against indecent and profane programming, the burden of pushing for further change in FCC regulations lies in the hands of the American people.

Sosta 10

Works Cited

"About the FCC." *fcc.* Federal Communications Commission, 28 Apr. 2008.

    Web. 18 May 2008.

Ahrens, Frank, and Lisa De Moraes. "FCC Throws Flag At CBS's Halftime

    Play; Commissioners Propose $550,000 Indecency Fine." *The*

    Washington Post. 23 Sept. 2004. *ProQuest.* Web. 18 May 2008.

Cantor, Joanne. "V-Chip." *Encyclopedia of Communications and Information.*

    Ed. Jorge R. Schement. Vol. 3. New York: Macmillan Reference USA,

    2002. *Gale Virtual Reference Library.* Web. 18 May 2008.

"FCC Regulation of Broadcast Obscenity, Indecency, and Profanity." Dow

    Lohnes PLLC, 2006. Web. 18 May 2008.

    <http://www.ucop.edu/irc/services/documents/indecencymemo.pdf>

"FCC V-Chip." *fcc.* Federal Communications Commission, 8 July 2003. Web.

    18 May 2008.

Hilgart, Art. "Stuff a Gag in the V-Chip." *Humanist* 57 (1997): 3. *Academic*

    Search Premier. Web. 18 May 2008.

McGregor, Michael A. "Regulation, Television." *Encyclopedia of Children,*

    Adolescents, and the Media. Vol. 2. Sage Reference, 2007. *Gale Virtual*

    Reference Library. Web. 18 May 2008.

Sosta 11

"Obscenity, Indecency & Profanity - Frequently Asked Questions." *fcc.*

Federal Communications Commission, 27 Apr. 2007. Web. 18 May

2008.

Simmons, Betty J., Kelly Stalsworth, and Heather Wentzel. "Television

Violence and Its Effect on Young Children." *Early Childhood*

Education Journal 26 (1999): 149–153. *Academic Search Premier.*

Web. 18 May 2008.

The following student sample, written by Ahmed Dessouki, is a response to the writing prompt "Discuss the definition of terrorism and how it relates to V from the movie *V for Vendetta*. In addition, discuss V's concept of revenge and liberty. Finally, connect these ideas to how he treats Evey Hammond as he attempts to 'cure' her." This particular prompt is focused. However, Ahmed still had to come up with an argument and support to defend his thesis. As you read, notice the different essay types in action. Also, you should notice the effective use of a counter argument. If you have seen the movie, you might consider how you would approach the same writing prompt.

Ahmed Dessouki

9 July 2008

One Man's Terrorist is Another Man's Freedom Fighter

What is terrorism? One would assume that all people can agree to the same definition. Unfortunately, this is not true! According to *Merriam-Webster Online Dictionary,* "Terrorism is the systematic use of terror especially as a means of coercion" ("Terrorism"). Here, "coercion" is the act of compliance under the act of terror. Terrorism is living in fear. This can be a result of the government's acts, a "crazy" person with any sort of weapons, or an intelligent man that utilizes any tools as a threat toward the government and society, forcing them to comply with his, or her, laws and demands. When looking at V's character, *V for Vendetta* is a movie that does not follow that definition of terrorism. He is not forcing the government to change, but he is asking for a whole new government.

As granted by the producers of the movie, Evey (played by Natalie Portman) has taken the leading role on screen. V is the second main character of the movie; however, almost every single second of the movie revolves around V's actions. After watching *V for Vendetta,* one can take note that V did not murder any innocent people, and he is not asking anyone to change their beliefs under the act of terror. Thus, V is not a terrorist. V states, "Justice and freedom are more than words. They are perspectives" (*V for Vendetta*). In

this quotation, the viewer can really understand V's "constitution." Another

quotation that lends credence to this is, "People should not be afraid of their

governments. Government should be afraid of their people" (*V for Vendetta*).

Both of these quotations clearly indicate V's beliefs, for he supports those

statements with his sequential line of actions. V's core values are to stand up

for what he believes in, fight until his last breath, and grant himself and the

people the justice that has been expunged. In addition, one can identify that V

is a man of honor, for he has a vision; a vision that every one of us should be

having and living by. It is a vision of principles and honorary systems that will

rule above anything that comes before it. This is a vision of freedom,

democracy, and justice. V is doing and accomplishing what every freedom

fighter is living, and dying for. The government should be working for the

people, as it is made and elected by the people. When governments forget

whom they are serving, chaos prevails.

Liberty, revenge, and justice are not just simple words. Men, women,

and children have died because of actions in the name of those words

throughout the history of mankind. V is trying to teach us the meanings of

those words, yet he proves how far he is willing to go to demonstrate the

blindness of the people when it comes to injustice and persecution. V states,

"There is something terribly wrong with this country, isn't there? Cruelty and injustice, intolerance and oppression" (*V for Vendetta*). V stands up for what he believes in; he sees that there is some change that needs to be done, and there is a clear message that he needs to carry to the people of England. However, he does not force the people to change, because that would define him as a terrorist. He uses his art of seduction to convince the people into believing his objectives by showing what the government is actually doing to its people, by stating personal experiences, and by demonstrating his vision in real events. V also declares, "I know why you did it. I know you were afraid. Who wouldn't be? War, terror, disease" (*V for Vendetta*). In V's opinion, the people's liberty is a right that has vanished from society. In this case, it can be interpreted as the people's freedom from fear.

Who decides what is right or wrong? The best way to address that question is by looking at the society's culture and history. V only kills the ones that made him into the person that he became; is that right or wrong? On whose book of judgment shall we decide the answer of this question? In addition, he kills the officers that follow those authority figures when they attack him. If we look at the civilized society, most of the people would say that violence is not the way that should be followed to handle any type of situation. This is a very valid argument, but what if there is no other way

Dessouki 4

because the government is corrupted in its way of upholding the law. V said, "Violence can be used for good" (*V for Vendetta*). Of course, not every problem requires actions such as the ones taken by V; however, these actions are inevitable when the time needs it. According to V, "There's no court in this country for a man like Prothero" (*V for Vendetta*). Prothero is a man who manipulated the system and is the cause of the death of thousands of people. The solution should be easy if someone reported him to the authorities; unfortunately, the chancellor is his accomplice. The highest figure of authority is the main traitor to his society. This is the time when civilians must step in to make things right once again, and this is what V is doing throughout his journey. For instance, this is what happened when the four fathers declared their independence from the British government. Today, nobody is calling them terrorists.

One might argue that V's acts are considered a terrorist's acts; however, the interpretation of this statement will change after analyzing V's acts more closely. First, V defends Evey when she is being attacked by actual government agents. Is that not heroic? Almost every woman in the world wants a hero like him to save her in that sort of position. Second, V destroys a statue, which did not result in the death of any civilians. Third, when delivering his speech, he alerts all people that he is going to blow up the parliament on November 5th the following year. That is not terror, for he is warning everyone before doing a certain action; one would be "stupid" to be near the parliament on that day of explosion. On the other hand, nobody had warned the United States of America a year before September 11th, 2001 that some group of people is going to blow up the twin towers in New York City. V takes matters into his own hands, but his actions carefully exclude him from being a "terrorist."

The biggest controversial argument is V's treatment of Evey in order to "cure" her. As a normal reaction to most people, V is cruel and "crazy" to torture Evey in such manner. But since when does treatment have to be painless? Chemo-therapy can answer this question, as it is one of the cures for some types of cancer. There is no objection there. Evey's sickness is fear, and she is the one who asked to be relieved of that fear. V knew the method and applied what he knew best; a personal experience that he, himself, had went through. Hence, he succeeds in his treatment, for Evey is cured and does not fear death. V is ingenious, and Evey actually thanks him at the end of the movie for what he has done for her. He has released her of her fear and made her free. It requires a lot of courage, strong will, and discipline to do what is necessary.

Dessouki 6

Mark Burgess, a center for defense information analyst, states, "Defining terrorism has become so polemical and subjective an undertaking as to resemble an art than a science" ("Terrorism: The Problems of Definition"). One could see that defining an ambiguous term can be very challenging, and Mark is right, because it is an art. Terrorism cannot be defined in one word, as people can argue all the time from all different points of views. However, one thing that is certain: V is not a terrorist. We have studied V's actions, behavior, reasoning, reaction, and personality. One would wish for more people such as V in our society, if and when the time asks for it. A better wish would be not to ever be in need of people like V, and to have a righteous, safe, and stable government as long as possible.

Works Cited

Burgess, Mark. "Terrorism: The Problems of Definition." *cdi*. Center for

   Defense Information, 1 Aug. 2003. Web. 12 Apr. 2009.

"Terrorism." *Merriam-Webster*. Merriam Webster Online, 2009. Web. 12 Apr.

   2009.

V for Vendetta. Dir. James McTeigue. Perf. Natalie Portman, and Hugo

   Weaving. 2006. Warner Bros, 2006. DVD.

The following student sample was written for a history class. Written by Randy Baviello, it is a response to the writing prompt "Discuss the modernization effort in Japan during the late nineteenth and early twentieth century. How was Japan able to modernize at such a rapid pace? Are there continuities between pre- and post-World War II Japan or does this period represent a break from the country's original modernization strategies?" As stated in the Introduction of this book, the techniques and strategies learned here can apply to other disciplines. In this essay, Randy combines many of the essay types to make an argument about Japan's history. Try to detect the different methods as you read. You should also notice the kinds of support Randy uses. In particular, Randy does not use quotes—he is summarizing the arguments written by other historians.

Randy Baviello

History 463B

Japan

The island nation of Japan endured an unprecedented modernization process during the latter half of the nineteenth century. From the end of Tokugawa reign in 1867 to the outbreak of the Russo-Japanese War in 1905, a sweeping political and economical revolution wracked the country resulting in Japan's emergence as a major player in global imperial competition. In some situations where massive change is initiated, civil war erupts, in others a cycle of repeated coups leads to unending instability. For Japan, these changes led to it becoming one of the most powerful nations on Earth. The unique aspect of the Japanese experience is that the changes were embraced at a higher societal level than is typical in modernizing societies. Japan's rapid modernization was only possible because its society was able to evolve at an equally rapid pace, thereby keeping up with the changing political, educational and economic landscape. By enduring the coming changes and being flexible enough to absorb them, Japan has continued to be a powerful nation to the present day.

The first area which saw massive alterations and facilitated modernization was the realm of politics and government. The Meiji Government, drawing on Western models introduced by European merchants and missionaries, created the foundation for a new, industrial society. Whenever a new regime initiates fundamental alterations to the fabric of a nation, the changes cannot endure without the adaptation and acceptance of its citizens. Even though Japan's political landscape was demolished and rebuilt again, its people accepted the challenge and found a way to work within the new framework. This is not to say there were not dissenters. Japan's revolution was a "revolution from above" in which the wealthy and educated samurai were responsible for the overthrow of the previous regime. Of course, there was not room at the top for all of them and some of the samurai were unhappy with the change in the status quo. The ultimate failure of the rebellion sparked by these disgruntled officials only strengthened the Meiji institution. Many samurai, along with the farmers in rural areas and the laborers in the cities, sought ways to make the situation work for them, unknowingly helping the society flourish as a whole.

The initial step taken towards political modernization was an effort to consolidate power in the central government. Daimyo were stripped of their lands and by 1876, the samurai were demoted from their lofty economic status. The numerous *han,* or political districts, were combined to form larger territorial units in the form of prefectures (Koin 314). This reorganization was certainly a crippling blow to many who were accustomed to life under rule of the shogun, especially the privileged samurai. The samurai, however, were highly educated and many were confident in their abilities to switch to alternate roles. In the rural countryside, one such man named Ishizaka Shoko rose to the challenge (Walthall 52). He was one who embraced the new governmental propaganda slogan "civilization and enlightenment" and in turn brought these ideas into the villages (Steele 63). Shoko worked to make the new institution benefit his village by emphasizing open discussion, justice and people's rights (Steele 63). Men like Shoko were instrumental in getting average citizens to accept and even embrace what was happening in Japan. He showed them a brief glimpse of what the new society could offer. This was an important accomplishment, because the same citizens would soon be realizing that with new freedoms in a society come new responsibilities.

One such responsibility came in the form of Imperial conscription which was instituted in 1873 (Aritomo 315). The importance of this move cannot be underestimated in analyzing Japan's successful modernization. Militaries were and still are important institutions in Western systems of government. In Japan's case, the Imperial Army was instrumental in fending off the samurai rebellions, thereby allowing the Meiji to continue in their reforms. By mandating military service, the government pulled men from every corner of the country and allowed them to broaden their horizons about

Baviello 4

their Japanese identity while simultaneously fostering a patriotic spirit. These characteristics were not inherent in Japanese society at the time, but were essential to the modernization effort (Gordon 67). Conscription was a tool which helped indoctrinate citizens in this concept. Once again, the crucial factor was that Japanese citizens accepted and adapted to the new responsibility. Being drafted was not always easy on families as is seen in the case of Nishimiya Hide whose son was drafted into the army during the Sino-Japanese war. This was a devastating blow which forced her to fend for herself economically and socially (Walthall 57). Hide, however, was able to maintain her family's shoe store through thrift and hard work. The citizens of Japan did not rebel over these conditions, but took them in stride and found ways to survive.

These specific changes made during Japan's modernization represent only a small part of the government's overall effort to reform the political system of the nation. They also highlight continuities that have run through the history of modern Japan. After World War II, citizens had to redefine their positions in a changed society, just as those living in the Meiji Era. A new government and a new constitution made it necessary to work within a different framework. Patriotic spirit has waxed and waned over the last 150 years, but was still present as Japan once again rose to world prominence during the postwar era. This is evidence of the flexibility of the Japanese people and their society as a whole.

The second area which was crucial to the modernization of Japan is the economy. The Meiji leaders in the 1870s understood that in order to rise to equality with the West, a vibrant and powerful economy was necessary. Slogans such as "rich country, strong army" permeated the lives of Japanese citizens as the government overhauled the country's financial systems and took steps toward industrialization. In the 1880s, Japan copied the European ideal of creating a national currency in the yen (Gordon 71). Land taxes were levied on individuals instead of being collected from villages thereby paving the way to massive public works projects (Gordon 71). These projects included dredging harbors and constructing railroads which in turn improved transportation and facilitated trade. Japanese society endured the harsh conditions present in an industrializing nation and eventually grew to enjoy the benefits provided by the outcome of becoming a modern nation.

One of the most important aspects of Japan's rapid economic modernization was the fledgling government's support of big business. During the 1870s, a great deal of attention was paid to training managers and drawing laborers into factories. By the 1880s, Japan possessed a strong wage labor force which is a necessary aspect of creating an industrial economy

Baviello 6

(Gordon 72). Although very little of the nation's initial industry was directly
financed by the Imperial government, (Gordon 71) European models were
examined and the move was made toward encouragement of smaller firms to
merge into large corporations (Eiichi 355). These large businesses, called
zaibatsus, learned to cut waste and reduce costs as markets became more
competitive and eventually became the cornerstone of Japan's economic might
(Iwasaki, "Mitsubishi and Japanese Coastal Trade, 1876" 358). This flexibility
trickled down into Japanese society as workers accepted fluctuating salaries
depending on the financial state of the company. This system was prevalent in
one of the more successful *zaibatsus,* the Mitsubishi Corporation (Iwasaki,
"Control of Mitsubishi, 1878" 358). This is not to say that conditions in the
factories were always pleasant and safe, but just as in the industrializing
phases of Europe and the United States, Japanese workers adjusted to the
challenges and pushed forward. Growing pains were inevitable as Japan
accomplished in twenty years what it took other nations almost forty years of
turmoil to produce.

　　With an industrial base in position, services began to improve. This is
another key element of modernization. An article on railroad manager
Kiroshita Yoshio's contributions highlights the increase in consumer
consumption by Japanese citizens in response to efforts made to attract their

business. While traveling abroad to Europe and the United States in 1899, Yoshio witnessed the politeness of railroad workers and how this increased business for their respective commuter rail companies (Ericson 121). Having nationalized the railroad system, the Japanese government viewed it as a valuable commodity for military purposes as well as a symbol of being a modern nation, but had neglected its use as a tool to improve the lives of the citizens. By adopting a "customer first" attitude and improving service, the railroad industry grew by leaps and bounds, eventually becoming a staple in the lives of common citizens (Ericson 116). There is little doubt that the success of this new approach influenced other industries to become friendlier to consumers which in turn stimulated the economy as a whole. The economy is a unique animal in which it feeds on itself. All the factories and workers in the world are useless without customers to buy their products. By increasing the quality of the product, revenue grew and workers receive higher compensation. Higher paid workers had more money to inject back into the cycle. For this reason, the evolution of Japanese society's increasing demands for better value of consumed goods and services was instrumental to the success of its modern economy.

Little has changed in the present day regarding economic issues in Japan. The government still supports big business and also played an important role in the "economic miracle" of the postwar era. The fiscal

policies of the Meiji era laid the groundwork for a strong national currency

which is still in use today and the industrial base, created over a hundred years

prior, allowed Japan to enjoy unprecedented commercial success in the 1970s

and 80s. Yoshio's groundbreaking work in the railroad sector eventually led to

what is now one of the most robust transportation systems in the world. His

attention to improving both service and product quality began a legacy which

has been a hallmark of Japanese industrial power and of an economy whose

products are lauded worldwide as being among the finest in the world.

Although the government acted as a catalyst for Japan's success in rapidly

modernizing its economy, it is important to recognize that the Japanese society

as a whole made vital contributions and sacrifices which made this situation

possible. Without patience and flexibility as a people, this goal could not have

been achieved.

The next area which was improved in order to facilitate rapid

modernization was education. The Meiji leaders believed that Japan must

become an equal to the Western powers in all aspects. They realized that the

source of the wealth and influence enjoyed by the West stemmed from their

devotion to mass education. It was decided that Japan must do the same to be

competitive. This was not as difficult to implement as other ideas, due to the fact that the former samurai were the bureaucrats running the government. Historically the samurai class was the most educated in Japanese society and supported the spread of learning throughout the lower classes. They understood that it would take more than just a handful of educated men to achieve their goals in such a timely manner, so they set to work improving educational methods and institutions. In 1890, the emperor released the "Imperial Rescript on Education" which became an important tool used by the government to accomplish its mission of creating a uniform, compulsory system of schooling. It served as a powerful indoctrinating agent for the modernizing Japanese society (Eifu 343). In less than thirty years, the Meiji institution had overhauled and expanded education in Japan and in doing so taken large strides toward modernization.

Revamping the school system was essential to providing education for future generations however it was not enough to provide an adequately trained workforce in the late nineteenth century. The government knew that it would have to break down the virtual political walls Japan had built around itself. It accomplished this by sending citizens abroad to retrieve knowledge from other nations (Gordon 73). This knowledge came not only in the form of book learning, but also in the understanding of Western attitudes, styles and the overall feel of a modern society. The first step taken by the Japanese government was the dispatch of the Iwakura Mission to the United States in 1871. Although the stated goal of this mission was to lobby for the revision of the unequal treaties, a task it failed miserably at, it also had the by-product of exposing important men to Western customs and technology (Lu 323). More importantly, the mission convinced these men that modernization was essential for a prosperous Japan in the future. Although the Iwakura mission was not an educational accomplishment typical to modernizing nations, it was absolutely vital to the success of Japan's new educational system.

The importance of education in Japanese society is reinforced by its prevalence in many stories about people during the Meiji period. Former samurai and rural leader Ishizaka Shoko stressed education to his children and his constituents as a basis for developing political awareness (Steele 62). Hatoyama Haruko was a product of various schools for girls in Tokyo, an experience which fueled her ambitious nature and propelled her to the highest echelons of Japanese society (Hastings 83). Jahana Noboru, an activist who promoted Okinawan rights, is an example of a man coming from humble beginnings whose education allowed him to rise to the forefront of politics on the small island (Smits 102–103). These three examples embody the deep penetration of the importance of education to Japanese society, regardless of status or gender. The sharp upturn in educational opportunity directly paralleled the increased rate of modernization experienced by Japan. It was an undeniable factor in the success of the modernization movement.

As in the previous two areas, continuities in the realm of education permeate modern Japan. The country today boasts a very robust school system and education is a key factor to economic and societal success. Japan is also inextricably linked to the rest of the world through its manufacturing and trade, two components which have facilitated the current trend toward globalization. Although very isolated in the mid-nineteenth century, Japan has placed continued emphasis on expanding its horizons by borrowing concepts from abroad and internalizing them with the end product generally being unique and very profitable. This system comes as a result of Japanese society's efforts to draw its small nation into the global spotlight. Although some rural farmers or shortsighted individuals may have resisted the move towards broad education and the institution of Western ideas, the populace in general has embraced the concept and has made it a cornerstone of its society.

Continuities abound when comparing the modernization efforts of the Meiji period to the state of Japan in the present day. The most striking similarity, however, has been the flexibility shown by its populace in adapting to changing conditions. The drastic alterations made in the areas of politics, economics and education can be cited as responsible for the rapid

Baviello 12

modernization experienced, however without the support of the common

citizens at the grass roots level, the movement would have died in its infancy.

Governments led by repressive dictators have tried to stimulate quick

modernization in their nations with the hope of achieving similar results as

Japan, but none have been nearly as successful. Such a revolution is not

something which can be imposed on a populace, but rather must come from

within. Although every situation is unique, underdeveloped countries today

might want to emulate Japan in the late nineteenth century much the same as

Japan sought to emulate its Western counterparts during that time. Regardless,

the key still belongs with the average citizens, the ones who have the power to

make it happen.

Baviello 13

Works Cited

Aritomo, Yamagata. "Opinion on Military Affairs and Conscription, 1872."

    Japan: A Documentary History. Ed. David J. Lu. New York: M.E.

    Sharpe, 1997. Print.

Eifu, Motodo, and Inoue Kowashi. "Imperial Rescript on Education, 1890."

    Japan: A Documentary History. Ed. David J. Lu. New York: M.E.

    Sharpe, 1997. Print.

Eiichi, Shibuzawa. "Reasons for Becoming a Businessman, 1873." *Japan: A*

    Documentary History. Ed. David J. Lu. New York: M.E. Sharpe, 1997.

    Print.

Ericson, Steven J. "Kinoshita Yoshio." *The Human Tradition in Modern*

    Japan. Ed. Anne Walthall. Wilmington: Scholarly Resources, Inc.,

    2002. Print.

Gordon, Andrew. *A Modern History of Japan.* Oxford: Oxford University

    Press, 2003. Print.

Hastings, Sally A. "Hatoyama Haruko." *The Human Tradition in Modern*

    Japan. Ed. Anne Walthall. Wilmington: Scholarly Resources, Inc.,

    2002. Print.

Baviello 14

Iwasaki, Yataro. "Mitsubishi and Japanese Coastal Trade, 1876." *Japan: A Documentary History.* Ed. David J. Lu. New York: M.E. Sharpe, 1997. Print.

———. "Control of Mitsubishi, 1878." *Japan: A Documentary History.* Ed. David J. Lu. New York: M.E. Sharpe, 1997. Print.

Koin, Kido. "Replacing Han with Prefectures, Letter of Kido Koin, 1871." *Japan: A Documentary History.* Ed. David J. Lu. New York: M.E. Sharpe, 1997. Print.

Lu, David J. *Japan: A Documentary History.* New York: M.E. Sharpe, 1997. Print.

Smits, Gregory. "Jahana Noboru." *The Human Tradition in Modern Japan.* Ed. Anne Walthall. Wilmington: Scholarly Resources, Inc., 2002. Print.

Steele, M. William. "The Ishizaka of Notsuda." *The Human Tradition in Modern Japan.* Ed. Anne Walthall. Wilmington: Scholarly Resources, Inc., 2002. Print.

Walthall, Anne. "Nishimiya Hide." *The Human Tradition in Modern Japan.* Wilmington: Scholarly Resources, Inc., 2002. Print.

The following essay was written in response to "Is Wal-Mart's influence on society positive or negative?" In this case, two authors came together to do research and write the essay. As you read, notice how Kimberly Jasmin and Sheng Li try to convince you of their beliefs about Wal-Mart. What techniques do they use throughout the essay? How effective is their use of support within each paragraph? How would you answer this writing prompt?

Kimberly Jasmin

Sheng Li

English 1C

Wal-Mart: Business as Usual

Wal-Mart is known to be one of the most successful and well-known companies in the United States. Wal-Mart "operates in 44 countries, has 2,276 stores outside of the U.S. and has more than 100,000 associates in Mexico alone, and does $56.3 billion in sales oversee" (Malone). However, customers today do not stop and think about where all of these numbers and facts come from. Based on research and other findings, Wal-Mart promotes that they "sell for less" and assures "satisfaction guaranteed" (Kuhlken 70). Also, to achieve these kinds of revenues, Wal-Mart has stores located not only in America, but also in many other countries, including Bangladesh and China. However, by investigating their ways of doing business and by following their success of expanding their multi-billion dollar franchise, it can be proven that Wal-Mart profits from their immoral behaviors and thus, have a negative influence on today's society worldwide. It is important to inspect their business ethics; for that reason, they will use the money that they saved from child labor and/or sweat shops to give their customers the ultimate low prices they are looking for. As a result of this, the people working for Wal-Mart are the ones who are made to suffer.

How might one define the words "negative" and "influence"? In the *New International Webster's Standard Dictionary,* the term "negative" is defined as "lacking any affirmative quality" (194). Also, in the same dictionary, the term "influence" means "a power that effects, an effect shaped by control or persuasion" (150). Likewise, to better understand these terms, the *Doubleday Dictionary* further states that the term "negative" means "containing contradictions or characterized by denial or refusal" (484). In addition, *Doubleday Dictionary* says "influence" is characterized as a "power arising from social, financial, moral, or similar authority" (368). Thus, after reviewing a few definitions, it can be concluded that the terms "negative" and "influence" is someone or a group of people who have money and power to persuade other people, and yet, they still have contradictions and denials upon examining their work ethics. Therefore, Wal-Mart, the world's leading retailer, is affecting society in a negative way.

In spite of their negative affect, some customers are blind to the truth—all they see are low prices. Although Wal-Mart is known to be one of the biggest retailers in the world, how do they continue to profit while selling items for lower prices than their competitors? It can be said that Wal-Mart profits from their welcoming services, excellent merchandise, and affordable prices. As their slogan says "always low prices," it provides a friendly and heart-warming message to the families around the world. Although they do seem to have good business morals and family oriented services, Wal-Mart also profits from their employees by taking advantage of them with their health care system. According to an online article, Debbie Shank, a former Wal-Mart employee, got into a car accident with a trucking company in May 2000. Her husband, Jim Shank, sued the trucking company for $1 million dollars and after all legal fees were paid, she only had $417,000 left over. Wal-Mart wanted the money that the Shank family won in the legal court case and because of it, Debbie Shank and her family lost the money to pay for her medical expenses. Jim Shank, who was appalled and stunned, firmly asks, "'Who needs the money more? A disabled lady in a wheelchair with no future, whatsoever, or does Wal-Mart need $90 billion, plus $200,000?'" (Kaye). In this case, it clearly shows how Wal-Mart is avaricious for more money; however, it seems unethical and unjust for a big-shot company to take money from a person who really needed it the most. Thus, since money is a norm worldwide, it has a negative influence on people who are under Wal-Mart's heath care coverage either here in America or those in other countries. As a result, this incident shows how the Wal-Mart Corporation is superior to their "associates" who work for Wal-Mart.

Although they collect billions of dollars each year, Wal-Mart's "moral practices" are corrupt. It is evident that Wal-Mart has a brilliant production plan as well as skilled employees to assist the consumers. However, this is not always the case. For example, Wal-Mart has been known to use and train illegal immigrants as part of the cleaning crew that work at night. According to one article, the Associated Press states that "two senior Wal-Mart Stores, Inc. executives knew cleaning contractors were hiring illegal immigrants . . . [in which they] slept in the back of the stores" ("Wal-Mart Execs Knew of Illegal Workers, U.S. Says"). Based on this article, illegal immigrants were being hired to perform cleaning tasks, and perhaps they were paid lower than minimum wage. In addition, Wal-Mart agreed to pay a sum of "$11 million" to settle the case; however, "top" executives claim that they did not know or encourage the practices. The conflict is why would Wal-Mart want to hire illegal immigrants to clean up the stores they supposedly did not know about? It is ironic how "top" executives did not know about the practices because they are responsible for most of the work that happens within their stores. Furthermore, in a testimony by Wal-Mart, it was discovered that the executives did know of the incident; however, they tried to hide it from investigators by using bribes. According to the same article, it states, "The sworn testimony established that top Wal-Mart executives conspired with contractors to exploit undocumented immigrants" ("Wal-Mart Execs Knew of Illegal Workers, U.S. Says"). There is no doubt that Wal-Mart has contradictions in their claims. The fact that they said they did not know of the act, but then agreed to pay for the case shows how hypocritical the company can be. Consequently, Wal-Mart "influenced" the investigators with money to persuade them to drop the case. Therefore, Wal-Mart is not only the world's largest retailer, they are also the world's biggest liars who hired "undocumented immigrants" to clean up their store. As a result, Wal-Mart is throwing its money around to let people know that they have the power to manipulate federal investigators by "influencing" them with money to hide their dishonest deeds.

In addition to these "shady" practices, where else can Wal-Mart cut corners in order to profit? The answer to that question is that Wal-Mart also takes money away from cities and puts small town stores out of business. In the *Gale Encyclopedia of U.S. Economic History,* it states, ". . . independent store owners often went out of business when Wal-Mart came to town . . ." ("Wal-Mart Stores" 1071). Additionally, Wal-Mart transferred thousands of "Main Street" stores and had an expansion plan targeted at small town communities, especially near suburban areas, to supposedly help the market in that area. (Hawkins 368; Kuhlken 70). However, Tina Gianoulis, the author of "Wal-Mart" in *Bowling, Beatniks, and Bell-Bottoms: Pop Culture of*

20th-Century America, firmly says, ". . . the presence of Wal-Mart takes business away from downtown areas and therefore weakens the entire town" (804). If Wal-Mart wanted to help a community, why would they drive small town stores out of business? It seems unethical for a well-known company to force these small stores to go elsewhere (in most cases, they simply close because there is no other place to go). Instead of helping the community make money, Wal-Mart actually influences other stores, causing those stores to lose money and close. Although it might be the nature of a capitalist society, this kind of competition is unhealthy and unbalanced.

Not only does Wal-Mart have allegations toward dishonest ways of making money, but they also partake in the use of child labor. In two articles, it states that a "code would prohibit the use of child labor . . . [however,] the consumer may discover that the shirt from the most competitive retailers were made using child labor" (Mandle 96; Handelman and Arnold 35). Moreover, Wal-Mart also emphasizes that if the U.S. will approve labor laws, they [U.S.] will lose investments ("Gap, Mattel, Speedo, Wal-Mart Products Linked to Child and Sweatshop Labor in China and India"). Additionally, another online article states that "Wal-Mart Inc., the world's largest retailer, will pay $135,540 to settle federal charges that it broke child labor laws" ("Wal-Mart Settles Child Labor Cases"). Apparently, Wal-Mart assigned underage workers to use hazardous equipment such as chain saws, paper bailers, and fork-lifts in Arkansas, Connecticut, and New Hampshire; however, the Child Labor Law prohibits anyone under eighteen years old from operating hazardous equipment ("Wal-Mart Settles Child Labor Cases"). Wal-Mart denied these accusations. On the other hand, they were still willing to pay for the penalty. Also, their payment may seem offensive to the consumers because if their underage employees were to get hurt, Wal-Mart will just pay the employees to keep quiet, and maybe their injuries will stay hidden from the public. In addition, Wal-Mart also enforces children to fabricate their products. According to Bill Quinn, the author of *How Wal-Mart is Destroying America and the World,* states that "Wal-Mart defines 'child labor' as work by children under the age of fourteen; after that age, apparently, they're considered fully capable of the 'maximum tolerance' fourteen-hour days and seventy-two hour weeks" (92). As stated by Quinn, Wal-Mart has the power to determine whether or not a child is capable to work the "full-time" schedule. Wal-Mart should be put under surveillance to detain the usage of child labor in the future. Yet again, Wal-Mart is using their "influences" to persuade the Child Labor Officials in a "negative" way. Clearly, Wal-Mart did not have any concerns for their underage workers because all they wanted was to increase their sales by blackmailing their own country.

There are other ways Wal-Mart brings lower prices to their customers. If the clothes or merchandise they buy are made outside America, the price per item is usually cheaper. Wal-Mart encounters many allegations toward their company including sweatshops in other countries. To further advance this claim, Jay M. Handelman and Stephen J. Arnold, the authors of "The Role of Marketing Actions With a Social Dimension: Appeals to the Institutional Environment," strongly agree as they say, ". . . [Wal-Mart] buys from overseas sweatshops or has been charged with engaging in deceptive advertising and pricing practices" (37). Furthermore, customers do not realize that the clothes that are from these Wal-Mart stores are actually produced from other countries around the world using sweatshops. An example of sweatshop accusation is in Bangladesh. When customers purchase a shirt from Wal-Mart, do "'[they] ever imagine young women in Bangladesh forced to work from 7:30 A.M. to 8:00 P.M., seven days a week, paid just 9 cents to 20 cents an hour . . .?'" (Robbins 87). Thus, Wal-Mart gets lower prices from other countries as it helps increase their profit margin and saves them money. However, they fail to consider those who work in sweatshops more than twelve hours a day, seven days a week.

Furthermore, Wal-Mart suppliers in China are also not providing enough resources for their workers. According to an article, the Associated Press mentions "Several Chinese suppliers of Wal-Mart Stores Inc. fail to

Jasmin, Li 9

legally require wages or provide health insurance and allow poor working conditions" ("Wal-Mart's China Suppliers Underpay"). Moreover, managers at two companies cited in the report denied the accusations, but the China Labor Watch said that some suppliers were paid as little as half of the minimum wage, required them to work overtime, and one company only provided a single restroom for 2,000 employees ("Wal-Mart's China Suppliers Underpay"). Based on this information, many employees are clearly not getting the fair and proper benefits they should be getting as associates. Instead, Wal-Mart Corporations are taking their employees' skills for granted to further expand the company. Instead of accommodating their workers with adequate wages and work conditions, Wal-Mart charges workers "one hour's pay for being one minute late to work, are overdue in paying back wages and have threatened to fire those who fail to work overtime" ("Wal-Mart's China Suppliers Underpay"). By cheating innocent people into working, Wal-Mart's profits continue to rise as the innocent Chinese workers continue to make two Yuan, which is equivalent to twenty-five U.S. cents per hour in which they are supposed to be paid four point sixty-six Yuan, which is equivalent to fifty-eight U.S. cents ("Wal-Mart's China Suppliers Underpay"). The ability to buy merchandise from overseas for a few cents, then re-sell it in America for a few dollars continues to work for Wal-Mart—they are the number one retailer in the world. But these business practices come with a price. The individuals who work for Wal-Mart, those who actually do the work, do not benefit from the billions made by their company.

By further examining all of their iniquitous claims, it can show how Wal-Mart rises from their immoral behaviors. For example, Quinn states, "It would be a complete violation of our policy for anyone to participate in any charade that would merely make a pretense of observing a thorough inspections" (94). However, when there would be an inspection of the factories, there would be announcement dates that allowed the managers to have plenty of time to cover up or hide their evil practices (Quinn 92). Additionally, the author further adds "factory managers had 'trained workers to answer prepared questions and paid them a bonus for remembering them correctly during visits by Wal-Mart inspectors" (Quinn 92). According to Quinn, managers from various Wal-Mart stores required their workers to remember "prepared questions and answers" so that the inspectors will be tricked into believing that the employees worked under good working conditions. Wal-Mart, once more, used their money to "influence" their own associates to stay quiet if they were questioned by the inspectors. In addition, by promoting sweatshops and other unfair working conditions, it leads the consumers to believe that the products were made in excellent working

Jasmin, Li 11

environments, because when they do get monitored, they would pick their own loyal Wal-Mart investigators so that there would not be any surprise examinations (Greenhouse 2). This is just another unethical business practice used by Wal-Mart. For Wal-Mart, this kind of immoral behavior would be "business as usual."

Upon examining these examples of Wal-Mart and its affect toward society worldwide, it can be said that the underlying message they portray is that they are a well-known company that could do whatever they want because they have the power. Wal-Mart and their selfish acts show that money plays a big role in their pursuit of this power. Wal-Mart should not take advantage of overseas workers in Bangladesh or China because those workers deserve to be treated equally while working for the world's largest retailer store. Moreover, Wal-Mart should not abuse their power by using profit to persuade others into believing that Wal-Mart's work ethic. Instead, Wal-Mart should use their profits to help pay higher wages and provide acceptable working conditions, store environments, and healthcare for those who really need it. Thus, if Wal-Mart does not change their immoral and dishonest ways of doing business, the public will eventually stop shopping at Wal-Mart. If, and when this happens, Wal-Mart will be forced to change their "evil" ways.

Jasmin, Li 12

Works Cited

"Gap, Mattel, Speedo, Wal-Mart Products Linked to Child and Sweatshop
Labor in China and India." *Democracy Now!* Democracy Now! The
War and Peace Report, 30 Oct. 2007. Web. 30 July 2008.

Gianoulis, Tina. "Wal-Mart." *Bowling, Beatniks, and Bell-Bottoms: Pop
Culture of 20th-Century America.* Ed. Sara Pendergast and Tom
Pendergast. Michigan: UXL, 2002. 802–804. Print.

Greenhouse, Steven. "Plans to Curtail Sweatshops Rejected by Union." *Clean
Clothes Campaign.* Clean Clothes Campaign, 1998. Web. 15 July 2008.

Handelman, Jay M. and Stephen J. Arnold. "The Role of Marketing Actions
With a Social Dimension: Appeals to the Institutional Environment."
Journal of Marketing 63.3 (1999): 33–48. Print.

Hawkins, Richard A. "Wal-Mart." *Dictionary of American History.* Ed.
Stanley I. Kutler. 3rd ed. New York: Charles Scribner's Sons, 2003.
368. Print.

"Influence." *Doubleday Dictionary.* 1975. Print.

"Influence." *New International Webster's Standard Dictionary.* 2006. Print.

Kaye, Randi. "Brain-Damaged Woman At Center of Wal-Mart Suit." *cnn.com.*
Cable News Network, 2008. Web. 28 July 2008.

Jasmin, Li 13

Kuhlken, Robert. "Wal-Mart." *St. James Encyclopedia of Popular Culture.* Ed.
Sara Pendergast and Tom Pendergast. Michigan: St. James, 2000.
69–71. Print.

Malone, Robert. "Wal-Mart Takes Over the World." *msnbc.* Forbes, 2006.
Web. 27 July 2008.

Mandle, Jay R. "The Student Anti-Sweatshop Movement: Limits and
Potential." *Annals of the American Academy of Political and Social
Science.* 570 (2000): 92–103. Print.

"Negative." *Doubleday Dictionary.* 1975. Print.

"Negative." *New International Webster's Standard Dictionary.* 2006. Print.

Quinn, Bill. *How Wal-Mart is Destroying America and the World.* California:
Ten Speed Press, 2005. Print.

Robbins, Bruce. "The Sweatshop Sublime." *PMLA.* 117.1 (2002): 84–97.
Print.

"Wal-Mart Execs Knew of Illegal Workers, U.S. Says." *Los Angeles Times.*
Los Angeles Times, 8 Nov. 2005. Web. 7 July 2008.

"Wal-Mart Settles Child Labor Cases." *msnbc.* Associated Press, 12 Feb. 2005.
Web. 13 July 2008.

"Wal-Mart Stores." *Gale Encyclopedia of U.S. Economic History.* Michigan:
Gale, 2000. 1070–1071. Print.

Jasmin, Li 14

"Wal-Mart's China Suppliers Underpay." *msnbc.* Associated Press, 8 Dec.

2006. Web. 25 July 2008.

ACTIVITIES

Activities

1. **Types of Support:**

   Directions: The following support was written by Janelle Guzman in an essay about the causes and effects of bullying. For each piece of support, label the kind of support it represents. You should refer back to Chapter 1 and use the full name of the support.

   1. School bullying statistics show that "77% of students are bullied mentally, verbally, and physically" ("Bullying Statistics/Cyber Bullying Statistics/School Bullying Statistics").

      Type of Support?

      _____

      _____

      _____

   2. Ben Brennan discovered, "…the problem requires complete vigilance on the part of teachers…A computer database now records all reported incidents of bullying allowing teachers to examine and record the history and severity of cases and to take action accordingly."

      Type of Support?

      _____

      _____

      _____

3. According to Dr. Olweus, author of the book *Bullying in School: What We Know and What We Can Do,* "When bullying in school they have a strong need to dominate and subdue other students and to get their own way" ("Bullying in Schools").

   Type of Support?

   _____

   _____

   _____

4. Researchers have discovered, "the psychological stress can cause victims' bodies to be less resistant to disease and infection" ("Consequences of Bullying").

   Type of Support?

   _____

   _____

   _____

5. An example of a school shooting occurred in 1999 at Columbine High School. It is believed that the two boys, who shot twelve students and one teacher, were being bullied throughout school. The boys found it difficult to fit into cliques, and were often picked on by athletes and other students (Rosenberg).

   Type of Support?

   _____

   _____

   _____

3. **MLA Works Cited:**

Directions: Turn the following information into a proper MLA Works Cited. If the information involves a website, use the date you do the assignment as the "view date." When you are done, make sure everything is in alphabetical order. If you want to get the most out of this activity, you should type the Works Cited. If you need help, refer to Chapter 2 for guidelines.

1. Create a Works Cited entry for this book, the one you are using right now.
2. This is a book by Roy Morris Jr., called *The Better Angel: Walt Whitman in the Civil War.* This book was published by Oxford Press in New York in 2000.
3. This is a famous poem by Walt Whitman called "Crossing Brooklyn Ferry." However, it is from an online source. The name of the website is *Bartleby.com* and it is owned by a company called Bartleby.com with a copyright date of 2010.
4. This is the famous piece by Henry David Thoreau called "Civil Disobedience." In this case, the essay came from a book called *A World of Ideas,* 7th edition, and is published in New York by Bedford/St. Martins. This college textbook was published in 2006 and Thoreau's essay starts on page 137 and ends on page 157.
5. This is a movie on DVD called *District 9* and is directed by Neill Blomkamp. It stars an actor named Sharlto Copley. The movie was released in the theatre in 2009. Later that same year, Tri-Star Pictures released the movie on DVD.
6. In the December 7th, 2009, issue of *Time Magazine,* there is an article called "The Decade from Hell" written by Andy Serwer. It starts on page 30 and ends on page 38.
7. In a search for information on health care, you discover a website called *HealthReform.gov.* After reading the article titled "Preventing and Treating Diabetes: Health Insurance Reform and Diabetes in America," you discover that the website is owned by the U.S. Department of Health and Human Services, but the website has no copyright date and the article has no author.
8. In order to understand the word "hero," you search on *Dictionary.com* in order to discover the word's meaning. *Dictionary.com* is owned by Dictionary.com, LLC with a copyright in 2010.
9. This is a college textbook written by two authors, Jason McFaul and Eric MacDonald. The book is called *What a Trip* and is published by Kendall Hunt. The company is located in Iowa and the current edition was released in 2007.

10. This one will be challenging because there is no example in the book. Do the best you can with the information. You listen to a song called "Given to Fly" by a band named Pearl Jam. The song came from the CD titled *Yield*. The album was published by Sony Music Entertainment in 1998.

_____

_____

_____

_____

_____

_____

_____

_____

_____

_____

_____

_____

_____

_____

_____

_____

_____

_____

_____

4. **Sentence Meaning:**

In this activity, take each sentence(s) that contains a logic error in Chapter 16 and re-write a new sentence(s). Try to keep the meaning of your new sentence as close as possible to the original sentence. Some of these sentences are out of context, but do the best you can to make a new, coherent sentence.

_____

_____

_____

_____

_____

_____

_____

_____

_____

_____

_____

_____

_____

_____

_____

_____

_____

_____

_____

_____

_____

5. **Counter Arguments:**
   There are many student paragraphs and essays that appear in this book. Choose one and write a counter argument paragraph in response to the student's assignment. Even if the essay you choose already has a counter argument, you can write another paragraph that continues the counter argument.

_____

_____

_____

_____

_____

_____

_____

_____

_____

_____

_____

_____

_____

_____

_____

_____

_____

_____

6. **World View**—Understanding what you believe and why.

This activity is designed to help you think about how you view the world. Think critically about this question: How do you view the world? In other words, what is your opinion of society today? That is a huge question, and there are probably many things running through your mind right now. How does one even begin to answer that question?

Start by analyzing one of your core values. Can you apply it to how you feel about the world? In a paragraph or two, state your world view and analyze why you feel this way, or explain how you arrived at this world view.

Now that you have thought about some of your core values (we also call them foundations), look at some social issues. How do you apply what you believe to issues that people debate about on a regular basis? For example, how does your world view affect your opinion on capital punishment? Do you understand the underlying principals that made you arrive at your conclusion? You do not want to claim simply, "Capital punishment is wrong." You need to fully understand WHY you believe that to be true. If you were asked to write a research paper on this topic, understanding what you believe is very important. Once you understand the "WHY" you feel the way you do, you can begin constructing arguments. You can begin to convince your reader that your point of view is correct. You can begin to formulate an essay, using support and research, to help argue your claim.

_____

_____

_____

_____

_____

_____

_____

_____

_____

_____

_____

_____

7. **Peer evaluation for group activities.**

Peer evaluation occurs when you give a fellow student a copy of your essay in order to get comments and feedback. This process can be very important. It allows another person to read your draft and make comments. The goal is to improve your essay before the final version.

When doing peer evaluation, you want to say more than, "Yeah, I liked your essay." That does not help nor improve the essay. Instead, you want to give feedback that allows for improvement by making comments and using constructive criticism. If you like something, explain why. If you do not, you also need to explain why. But you also want to look for areas of improvement by making suggestions on how to fix things. Here is a list of suggestions to help in the peer evaluation process.

1. Identify the thesis. Does it make an argument and state why it is important? Do you recognize one of the three types of claims? What can you do to make it better?
2. Does the introduction present the topic using one or more of the methods discussed in this book? Does it have a theme or a hook to make you interested?
3. Are the supporting paragraphs adequately developed? Do they have support, such as examples or quotes? Does it follow the recommended style presented in this book? In other words, is there enough elaboration and analysis?
4. What is the draft's main strength? In other words, what does it do well? Compliment the student on something that was successful in the essay.
5. What is the draft's main weakness? In other words, what can be improved? This is where you make constructive criticisms in order to improve the rough draft.
6. Can you think of any counter arguments? In other words, are there things the student is not thinking about, or arguments that go against what he/she wrote? Are there additional arguments that you can think of that will help the student's argument?
7. Critique any other types of errors, such as paragraphs that are too short, sentences with errors, or anything that involves proofreading in order to improve the essay.

These seven things can be written down or discussed with the writer. Remember the goal: you want to help the other person become a better writer. In addition, by doing this, you will be exposed to different writing styles, which means you will be helping yourself every time you do peer evaluation.

8. **Self-evaluation: Analyzing your own essay:**

It is important to understand your own writing process. Once you have gone through the steps of writing an essay, you should evaluate what you did on that essay. By doing a self-evaluation, you will learn from your writing process. This experience is the key to improving your writing skills.

Answer the questions below. Try to be honest with yourself. Use what you have learned in this textbook to identify the different elements of your essay. Try to be conscious of what your strengths and weaknesses are in terms of your writing abilities. Answering these questions will help you become a better writer!

1. Look at your thesis. What kind of claim did you make? Why did you make this kind of claim?
2. Look at a supporting paragraph. What kind of support did you use? Give the actual name. Why did you use this support? Why was it effective?
3. How many drafts did you write? In other words, how many times did you proofread your essay and make changes to it? Did you have someone else proofread it?
4. How many hours (or minutes) did you spend doing research? How many sources are in your works cited? Could you have found more in order to make your essay stronger?
5. In terms of the essay type, do you feel you effectively used the strategies for this particular kind of essay in order to prove your argument? If not, what can be done better to help you use the strategies for specific kinds of essays?
6. What is the strength of the essay? In other words, what do you feel you did well on this assignment?
7. What is the essay's weakness? In other words, what do you feel you need to improve? What do you need help with?
8. Assign a grade to your essay. Do you feel this is an A, B, C, D, or F paper? Why? You can also use "+" and "−" as part of your evaluation. If your teacher uses a point value for grading, what score would you give your essay out of 100 points? Be honest.

_____

_____

_____

_____

_____

APPENDIX

Appendix

1. **The Ill Effects of the Five Paragraph Theme** by Kimberly Wesley

All of the techniques and strategies used in this book have prepared you to write more than five paragraphs in an essay. In fact, you should be able to write an essay no matter how many pages a professor assigns using as many paragraphs as you want in order to prove your thesis. Many instructors believe that teaching the traditional "five paragraph essay" structure stops students from developing a strong thesis—the "five paragraph essay" can limit creativity and critical thought in terms of writing an essay.

In the following essay, Kimberly Wesley argues that teaching the "five paragraph essay" can have negative consequences as students proceed through their academic career. As you read, note how Wesley constructs her arguments, uses support to prove her thesis, and argues solutions to the problems.

Wesley 1

The Ill Effects of the Five Paragraph Theme

Kimberly Wesley

In her 1973 poem, "A Work of Artifice," Marge Piercy considers the life of a

bonsai tree that "could have grown eighty feet tall / on the side of a mountain"

(3–4) but is, instead, "carefully pruned" to "nine inches high" (7–8). The

gardener, who controls the growth of the tree, "croons / . . . how lucky, little

---

Wesley 2

tree, / to have a pot to grow in" (11–16). Piercy's extended metaphor satirically compares the tree to a woman, the gardener to a representative of patriarchal society, and the pot to curlers, bound feet, and other methods by which society systematically judges and controls women. Had Piercy been alluding to the teaching of high school composition, she might have drawn parallels between the bonsai tree and the student writer, the gardener and the English teacher, the pot and the lock-step five paragraph theme (FPT). It is my contention that teachers of the five paragraph theme, like the representatives of patriarchal society, have become complacent in their acceptance of a tool that purports to nurture but, in fact, stunts the growth of human minds.

In the last ten years, *English Journal* has published numerous articles on composition instruction, but only two specifically address the five paragraph theme. In "Breaking the Five Paragraph Theme Barrier," university professor Thomas Nunnally is critical of students' reliance on the FPT, which he says has become a "national phenomenon," but concludes that if "a class's potential for improvement makes it impossible to accomplish more than teaching the barebones FPT, so be it" (68, 71). This kind of statement, which reinforces the status quo of high school composition instruction, is dangerous. In "Articulation and Student Voices," D. R. Randsell and Gregory Glau report findings from a survey of first-year college composition students who recommend that their high school English teachers quit "driving the 5-paragraph thing into our brains" and that "there must be more [types of essays] taught" (19).

As a teacher of English at a private secondary school, I have reflected critically on the five paragraph theme and the way in which this organizational format has come to be the standard for high school essay assignments. This past year I realized just how entrenched the FPT is in student minds. When a senior girl assigned to write a comparative analysis of two novels in seven-to-nine pages asked anxiously, "But how can I fit seven pages into five paragraphs?" a red flag went up. In my student's mind, the only kind of writing considered "good," the only kind of essay that would earn an "A" from the teacher, *must* have a thesis with exactly three points, no more, no less. As my student's query shocked me into realizing that one organizational format was being adopted wholesale by students, it also prompted me to reflect on how I design assignments and what I consider to be genuine growth in student writing. Do I consider a master of the five paragraph form a proficient writer, prepared for the demands of college? How has my past reliance on the FPT shaped my students' and my own views of writing? Has all my concern about the development of critical thinking been a lot of lip service? In this article, I examine the effects of the FPT on student learning and the conflict between my enforcement of the five paragraph theme and my conviction that writing is a rhetorical process.

Thomas Nunnally's definition of the five paragraph theme is useful here to establish common ground:

> As it is usually taught, the FPT requires (1) an introductory paragraph moving from a generality to an explicit thesis statement and announcement of three points in support of that thesis, (2) three middle paragraphs, each of which begins with a topic sentence restating one of the major ideas supporting the thesis and then develops the topic sentence (with a minimum of three sentences in most models), and (3) a concluding paragraph restating the thesis and points. (67)

In favor of this format, Nunnally points out that "the explicitness of the FPT—the discreteness of its parts and their functions—makes it practical to teach as well as eminently gradable" (68)—perhaps one of the reasons the FPT has become a "national phenomenon." On the other hand, Nunnally acknowledges the limitations of the form for anyone beyond Basic Writing at the college level, saying that the internalization of the FPT encourages writers to produce "bland but planned essays" (69). Nunnally even goes so far as to say that one student's "desire to fit the content of her paper into three neat little boxes" had "distorted" the purpose of the essay (70). By analyzing student essays I, too, find that the rigidity of the five paragraph theme actually dissuades students from practicing the rhetorical analysis necessary for them to become critical thinkers.

In my analysis of student texts, I have examined how the thesis statements of a particular five paragraph theme assignment reflect or do not reflect critical thought. For this article, I asked senior English students to do a comparative analysis of three texts—*The Odyssey, The Mayor of Casterbridge,* and *Dracula*—and to construct a controversial thesis statement that fits the three-pronged format (a daunting task!). My suggestion to them was to find one shared character trait and examine its causes or effects in each of the three books. What many of them came up with did satisfy the requirements of the three-pronged thesis. The following is one example: "In all three books, protagonists suffer from a permanent character flaw of excessive pride which causes them to be separated from loved ones, closed to new ideas, and absorbed in self-pity." Although this thesis follows the FPT format, it produces little analytical development within the body of the essay. The student spends the majority of each paragraph proving merely that the characters are, for example, separated from loved ones, rather than examining how pride causes them to become this way or why some consider a protagonist's separation from family a detriment to his/her status as a hero. The student touches on a more interesting train of thought at one point in the paper, suggesting that characters' insecurities ironically cause them to behave in a proud and defensive manner. The student does not expand on this idea, however, because it does not fit within the neat, prescribed formula of her thesis, which focuses only on the effects and not the causes of pride. Furthermore, had the student tried to develop this idea as her thesis, she may have found that insecurities cause only some characters to behave proudly. Moreover, she may have had a difficult time producing three distinct but equal causes of proud behavior. The result of my analysis of this essay (a valiant effort by my student) suggests to me that the thesis requirement of three separate but equal points hinders my student's thought process as she writes.

Other student writing samples carry seeds of critical thought that are never allowed to grow. In one written response to the same assignment, a student offers a vague thesis with book titles as points: "In *The Odyssey, The Mayor of Casterbridge,* and *Dracula,* the role of women within the novels is similar." Here the three-pronged thesis leads the student into a restatement of plot. Early in the introduction, however, the student says something that she does not explore anywhere else in the paper: "Each female protagonist shows a sense of strength which was not apparent in the presence of the men."

Inherent in this statement is a feminist critique. Had the student developed this line of thought in prewriting she may have been able to explore her own feelings as a woman in a male-dominated society and could have looked more deeply into the workings of patriarchy in each of the three books. She may not, however, have been able to divide her strong, central idea into three discrete points. Here again, the FPT's emphasis on organization over content squelches complex ideas that do not fit neatly into three boxes. Students' mere awareness that they must mold a topic to the FPT style inhibits their learning.

By doing textual analysis of student work, I have come to realize that my primary objection to the five paragraph theme is its tendency to stunt students' critical thinking abilities. Moreover, I have found the essays that best fulfill format requirements often turn out to be neatly packaged but intellectually vapid. A 1992 University of Hawaii study of student responses to writing assignments, including the FPT, reports similar findings:

> In structuring their arguments, [student writers] all wanted to exceed formulaic limits, but their teacher would allow no deviation. Clearly, whatever their instructor's intentions, these students were discovering thoughts and feelings through composing. And their discovery experiences proved incompatible with the prescribed essay structure. So the

students left the writing experience with considerable

frustration. (Marsella et al. 180)

Marsella et al. also conclude that students only challenge their own beliefs

when "their instructional contexts allow, even encourage, risk-taking" (185).

As a teacher assuming a rigid, artificial writing format for my students, I have

been limiting their ability to take intellectual risks and discouraging the kind

of learning that I believe only writing allows them to do.

Having recognized my error in inculcating students with the FPT, my

next question as a composition teacher is this: How do I create writing

assignments that encourage risk-taking and mental growth without letting good

organizational strategies go by the wayside? The answer is not, of course, to

turn to alternative methods of organization that presume to fit every writing

situation in the academy. These methods have just as much potential to become

"lock-step" as does the five paragraph theme. Rather, the answer is to revisit

the pedagogical theory with which I first embarked, starry-eyed, on teaching:

that every writing assignment poses a unique rhetorical problem. Viewed as

such, any writing assignment requires that writers first determine their purpose

and audience. Writers must question themselves as follows: What am I writing

about? Why am I writing about this topic? What do I know about this topic and

what do I still have to find out? What are my personal feelings on the matter?

Wesley 9

What effect do I want my writing to have on the reader? What is my reader's understanding of the issue? What biases or objections should I take into account? These questions are the most challenging ones for any writer and, unfortunately, the ones least often asked of high school students (and of ourselves in creating assignments). With a set "discourse" of writing (e.g., character analysis), a set topic (e.g., Iago), a set audience (e.g., the teacher), and a set organizational format (e.g., the five paragraph theme), students have to do very little rhetorical analysis and, as a result, rarely understand the purpose of their papers. As Richard Larson says in his 1992 critique of classes of discourse, high school English teachers too often ask students "to engage in what British educators refer to as a 'dummy run': an activity that has no purpose with identified readers but is designed to display the writer's ability to produce a frozen form" (32). However, if I, as an English teacher, give paper assignments that offer choices of purposes, topics, and audiences, I can prompt students to begin thinking rhetorically. After students have submitted a justification of their choices and answered the rhetorical questions listed above, we can talk as a class about effective methods of organization for sample rhetorical situations.

It is important to acknowledge here to those instructors who are loath to surrender the "practical to teach as well as eminently gradable" FPT

(Nunnally 68) that I am not suggesting that we abandon the principles of unity, coherence, and development that the five paragraph theme purports to teach. Rather, I suggest that we continue to teach the essay as a rhetorical form with three units—an introduction, a body, and a conclusion. By treating each of these parts as a rhetorical unit instead of a set number of paragraphs, we can approach student texts as records of their rhetorical problem-solving ability. It is vital that we teach students the purposes that each unit in an essay can serve. The introductory unit of the essay (which may be more than one paragraph, depending on the scope of the rhetorical problem) serves to grab the reader's attention, establish common ground, and define the problem and perhaps the process undertaken to solve that problem. The thesis (which most likely will occur either at the beginning or the end of the introductory unit—there are good models of both) states the writer's focus or position on the problem (without sub-points because—as seen in the above discussion—a rigid number of sub-points can inhibit student thought). The body unit of the essay should be an unspecified number of paragraphs, with each paragraph serving one of a variety of purposes: to define terms, to review the literature, to present evidence in favor of the thesis, to analyze that evidence, and to accommodate and/or refute opposing views. Finally, the concluding unit of the essay should serve to reassert the writer's position, to remind the reader of the importance to him/her of the problem at hand, and to pose questions on the issue that could be addressed by other writers. To help students attain an understanding of the purposes of these rhetorical units and make choices among them, we should analyze and critique papers written by college students in various discourses, articles written by journalists, and essays written by high school students. As Nunnally mentions in his article, doing rhetorical analysis of contemporary, professionally-written essays is a good way of giving students choices beyond the FPT (71). Moreover, critiquing these essays effectively helps students to see themselves as critical readers and to understand that the criteria for good writing are subjective and contextual.

In proposing that high school English teachers restructure their writing assignments, I am advocating a view of writing as a rhetorical process. If we accept this view, we cannot possibly continue assigning the five paragraph essay unless we simultaneously teach our students to critique it. Instead of teaching students to memorize a format and then manipulate every teacher-given topic to fit that format, we should ask students to reflect on what format best enables them to voice their concerns and meet the needs of their audience. In doing so, we encourage students to become communicators. If we do any less, we force students to continue as copiers of memorized form, denying them the freedom to think for themselves.

Works Cited

Larson, Richard L. "Classes of Discourse, Acts of Discourse, Writers, and

   Readers." *English Journal* 81.8 (1992): 32–36. Print.

Marsella, Joy, et al. "How Students Handle Writing Assignments: A Study of

   Eighteen Responses in Six Disciplines." *Writing, Teaching, and*

   Learning in the Disciplines. Eds. Anne Herrington and Charles Moran.

   New York: MLA, 1992. 174–88. Print.

Nunnally, Thomas E. "Breaking the Five Paragraph Theme Barrier." *English*

   Journal 80.1 (1991): 67–71. Print.

Piercy, Marge. "A Work of Artifice." *Circles on the Water.* New York: Knopf,

   1994. Print.

Randsell, D. R., and Gregory R. Glau. "Articulation and Student Voices:

   Eliminating the Perception that 'High School English Doesn't Teach

   Nothing.'" *English Journal* 85.1 (1996): 17–21. Print.

2. **Success in the classroom.**

Students always ask, "What can I do to get a better grade?" The answer(s) should not be a secret. The following list should be used as a tool and guideline to writing better essays and for succeeding in any class you might take.

DO

1. Do ask questions when you need something clarified.
2. Do proofread your essays. Or have a family member proofread for you, or a friend, or the writing center on your campus, or a tutor.
3. Do buy the *MLA Handbook.* Or know where to get the most recent MLA information.
4. Do read the entire chapter or entire reading assignment whenever a professor assigns something.
5. Do be prepared to talk about all the material you read for homework.
6. Do ask questions about any reading assignment (you should write out your questions as you do your reading).
7. Do raise your hand when a professor asks for a volunteer. Professors often remember those who volunteer and participate when they calculate grades at the end of the semester.
8. Do get to know the people around you. You never know when you will be absent.
9. Do know how to correctly format your essay in the word processing program you are using.
10. Do communicate with your professors, especially if there are problems affecting your abilities in the classroom. This includes illness, handicaps, and medications you might be taking.
11. Do yourself a favor and buy a computer and printer. Having a computer at home will make research and essay typing much easier. The campus also has computers and printers available for you to use if you do not have a computer at home.
12. Do think critically about the world.

Index

activities, 369
anthology, 24
argument, 49, 259

books, 7, 23
brainstorm, 39
    cluster, 40
    freewrite, 41
    listing, 39
    outline, 42

Cause and Effect, 211
censorship, 281, 317
claims, 49
    of value, 49
    of policy, 50
    of fact, 50
Compare and Contrast, 147
conclusion, 97
contractions, 293
counter argument, 260
cross-reference, 28
culture, 169

Definition, 129
depression, 199
dictionary, 25

ellipses, 19
essay, 111–288
evaluation, 381
    peer, 381
    self, 383

fallacy, 213, 297–301
first person, 292
formality, 291

Internet, 9, 26
interpretation, 4–5, 6
introduction, 65

Japan, 337
journals, 8, 25

literature, 237

MLA, 15
    format, 15–16, 291–292
    in-text, 16
    Works Cited, 23

paragraphs, 65–100
    introduction, 65
    support, 81
    conclusion, 97
    counter argument, 260–263
    refute, 260–263
Problem and Solution, 179
Process Analysis, 111
proofreading, 294

quotations, 16

refute, 260

school,
   dishonesty, 231
   private, 161
   public, 161
   success in the classroom, 399
   uniforms, 273
second person, 292
sentence meaning, 297
slang, 293
support, 3–5, 81

terrorism, 329
thesis, 49
timed writing, 303
transitional phrases, 84–85, 261

Wal-Mart, 352
Wesley, Kimberly, 387